2004 PO

GW00692291

ONG
A RHYME

IMAGINATION FOR
A NEW GENERATION

Eastern England
Edited by Steve Twelvetree

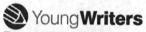 Young**Writers**

First published in Great Britain in 2004 by:
Young Writers
Remus House
Coltsfoot Drive
Peterborough
PE2 9JX
Telephone: 01733 890066
Website: www.youngwriters.co.uk

SB ISBN 1 84460 556 6

Foreword

Young Writers was established in 1991 and has been passionately devoted to the promotion of reading and writing in children and young adults ever since. The quest continues today. Young Writers remains as committed to engendering the fostering of burgeoning poetic and literary talent as ever.

This year's Young Writers competition has proven as vibrant and dynamic as ever and we are delighted to present a showcase of the best poetry from across the UK. Each poem has been carefully selected from a wealth of *Once Upon A Rhyme* entries before ultimately being published in this, our twelfth primary school poetry series.

Once again, we have been supremely impressed by the overall high quality of the entries we have received. The imagination, energy and creativity which has gone into each young writer's entry made choosing the best poems a challenging and often difficult but ultimately hugely rewarding task - the general high standard of the work submitted amply vindicating this opportunity to bring their poetry to a larger appreciative audience.

We sincerely hope you are pleased with our final selection and that you will enjoy *Once Upon A Rhyme Eastern England* for many years to come.

Contents

Katherine Burchell (9)	20
Cseperke Asztalos (10)	20
Toby Wright (9)	21
Joshua Course (10)	21
Conor O'Brien (7)	22
Melissa Scott (9)	22
Michael Holland (9)	22
Francesco Beber Fraser (8)	22
David Wilson (9)	23
Stephen Smith (8)	23
Joanna Perera (8)	23
Danielle Smith (8)	24
Rhea Andrews (9)	24
Rebecca Shevlane (8)	24
Christopher Scott (8)	25
Alice Duncan	25
Jack Kempton (9)	25
Amanda Moller (10)	26
Luke Perera (10)	26
Vicky Chalmers (10)	27
Victoria Nicholls (7)	27
Georgina Emery (9)	27
Claire Sharp (9)	28
Ewan Wilson (10)	28
Charlie Dean (7)	28
Meitar Blumenfeld (10)	29

Gresham Village School, Norwich

Sabina-Maria Zappia (10)	29
Natalie Kinsley (10)	30
Holly Wright (11)	30
Jennifer Holt (11)	31
Charlie Fiddian (10)	31
Joanna Annison (10)	32
Jessie Kellock (10)	32
Theo Young (10)	32
Lucy Hardy (11)	33
Florence Blyth (10)	33
Jonathan Hayman (10)	33

Lee Chapel Primary School, Basildon

Chris Reed (8)	34
Rebecca Smith (8)	34
Timothy Churchill (8)	35
Misha Towler (8)	35
Taylor O'Neill (8)	36
Brooke Saunders (8)	36
Christopher Johnson (10)	37
Lucie Frater (8)	37
Robert Scowen (8)	38
Melih Manyera (8)	38
Sohaib Ahmad (9)	39
Sam Carmichael (9)	39
Nathan Connor (9)	40
Jessica Moss (9)	40
Hayley Chrystie (8)	41
Molly Dowling (9)	41
Chloe Fowler (8)	42
Charlie Boshell (8)	42
George Hunt (9)	43
Kieran Eldridge (9)	43
Harry Gadlin (9)	44
Peter Bines (9)	44
Lois Mensah-Afoakwah (8)	45
Apphia Williams (9)	45
Aamna Khan (10)	46
Devon Barr (9)	46
Leanne Warren (10)	47
George Case (8)	47
James Genes (9)	48
Steven Le Count (8)	48
Courtney Wardell (8)	49
Emma Beard (8)	49
Ebony Lynn (8)	50
Alexander Bird (9)	50
Megan Williams (10)	51
Mitchell Wilk (9)	51
Zahraa Ejaz (8)	52
Michael Lynch (8)	52
Craig Hookings (9)	53
Adam Summerfield (8)	53

Megan Cleverley (9)	54
Lauren Borley (8)	54
Amber Thurlow (8)	54
Zoë Hales (11)	55
Joe Ludlow (8)	55
Amy Cantwell (8)	55
Heather Springer (10)	56
Charlotte Woods (10)	56
Gregg Mint (9)	57
Mariam Khan (9)	57
Arron Armiger (9)	57
Molly Mackay (7)	58
Rebecca Lewis (8)	58
Jodi O'Sullivan (8)	58
Madeline Turner (8)	59
Abbi Potts (8)	59
Jacey Ritchie (8)	60
Becca Ingledew (8)	60
Morgan Sprules (7)	60
Luke Townsend (9)	61
Jamie Miln (9)	61
Amy McCormick (9)	62
Hannah Jeffrey (10)	62
William Sartain (9)	63
Megan Mackay (10)	63
Clark Howe (8)	63
Lauren Claxton (10)	64
Rachel Brown (9)	64
Nicole Fowler (10)	65
Amiee Townsend (9)	65
Billie-May Colverson (11)	66
Alexandra Esme Knox (8)	66
Michael Bird (7)	66
Natalie Reynolds (10)	67
Nicholas Fulton (9)	67
Jamie Robertson (9)	67
Kirsty Wood (10)	68
Connor Randall (11)	68
Kelly Burdett (10)	69
Daniel Hawkins (10)	69
Katie Bird (10)	70
Abbie Fry (10)	70

Beth Burnet (10)	71
Alice Bannon (9)	71
Christie Lee (10)	72
Thomas Bakasa (9)	72
Marina Mensah-Afoakwah (10)	73
Michael Christian (10)	73
Reece Hendy (10)	74
Amy Prankard (10)	74
Whitney Billett (10)	75
Sam Spriggs (10)	75
Nick Gardner (11)	76
Charlotte Toms (10)	76
Ashley Brown (11)	77
Lauren-Rose Major (9)	77
Georgia Savage (11)	78
Benjamin Morris (8)	78
Nathan Blackwell (10)	78

Marsh Green Primary School, Dagenham
Lily Wu (8)	79
Ruth Muleya (9)	79
Lakhvinder Singh (8)	79
Luigi Kongo (9)	80
Jack Heywood (9)	80
Harrison Smith (8)	80
Taylor Furneaux (8)	81
Liam Baker (8)	81

Riverside Junior School, Hullbridge
Katherine M Ellis (8)	81
Alex Thraves (8)	82
Robert Vine (9)	82
Sashenka Levey (11)	83
Sophie Goodliffe (11)	83
Samantha Tautz (8)	83
Paige Ruskin (10)	84
Luke Smith (9)	84
David Green (10)	85
Andrew Gilbey (10)	85
Ryan Hirst (7)	86
Daniel Cole (11)	86

James Wood (10)	87
Adam Rice (7)	87
Joe Hall (8)	88
Louise Turner (9)	88
Amanda Ambrose (9)	88
Alice Baker (9)	89
Chantelle Ann Hand (10)	89
Amy Jones (11)	90
Connor Clift (7)	90
Lauren Bibby (9)	91
Melissa Keene (7)	91
April Byott (9)	92
Lucy Williamson (9)	92
Dermot Dobson (10)	92
Jessica Monk (8)	93
Elysia Anthony (8)	93
Lewis Groombridge (8)	93
Taylor Gouldsmith (9)	94
Beth Goessen (8)	95
Dean Bonning (8)	95
Jodie Whittington (9)	96
Katy Brown (8)	96
Robin Mead (9)	97
Jordan Swinge (7)	97
Megan Smith (8)	98
Holly Williams (8)	98
Connor Baker (10)	98
Harry Cole (8)	99
Jason Jones (8)	99
Chelsie Benson (7)	99
Nicole Clayden (10)	100
Ryan Beckwith (7)	100
Bonnie Degenhard (7)	100
Emily Pearson (11)	101
George Flanagan (11)	101
Hayley Deeks (8)	102
Kim Radmore (11)	102
Ella George (10)	103
Georgia Davies (8)	103
Nathan Adewunmi (8)	103
Sonny Horwell (8)	104
Keye Frith (7)	104

Adam Tucker (9)   148
Paul Oliphant (10)   149

St Mary Magdalen Primary School, King's Lynn
Vicky Eves (10)   149
Jake Fenn (9)   150
Jodie Button (10)   150
Daryl Waters (9)   151
Katherine Jones (10)   151
Jamie Marks (10)   152
Jamie Hart (10)   152
Rebecca Gipp (11)   153
Max Rossiter (11)   153
Jake Reed (10)   154
Ross Lucie-Smith (11)   154
Holly Eastwood (10)   155
Katy Flett (9)   155
Daniel Rains (11)   156

Sacred Heart Convent School, Swaffham
Morgan Creed (11)   156
Rosalind Peters (11)   157
Amy Stevens (11)   158
Beccy Case (11)   158
Bronwen Brewer (11)   159
Sophie Prentis (10)   159
Sarah Johnson (11)   160
Megan Hook (10)   160
Sophie Morgan-Short (10)   161
Emily Chaffer (11)   161
Hannah Coggles (10)   162

Wimbotsham Primary School, King's Lynn
Alice Harness (9)   162
Holly Bloy (10)   163
Fiona Thompson (11)   163
Ellen Atkinson-Legge (9)   164
Alex Grant (10)   164
Liam Thorpe (10)   165

The Poems

The Demons

They ran,
They charged,
Their single goal,
Was to destroy all.

Their task that lay ahead
Was simple
Yet risky,
It was to wreck.

It was to stop,
To kill,
To not care,
To take even death's life away.

These beasts
These monsters
Could not, would not
Be destroyed.

They were solely made out of evil
Their evil would pierce
Even the bravest man's heart,
Only joy could destroy them.

In the end
They'll stand no longer
We will defeat them
In the future.

Laurie McGeoghegan (11)
Girton Glebe Primary School, Cambridge

The Garden

The plants grow in the soil and the trees do too.
Making the garden look pretty they do.
Statues standing everywhere looking just like you.
The plants grow in the pots.
The wind blows through the trees and the well is near.

Jared Griffiths (7)
Girton Glebe Primary School, Cambridge

When Daddy Fell Into The Pond

Everyone was feeling grumpy
The pie for tea was lumpy
So Mummy said, 'Let's go outside for some fun'
'Yes,' cried the children, 'we could do with a run.'

The children started to play with the hose
Suddenly they began to have a humongous fight
'*Stop! Stop!*' shouted Mummy. 'What's going on here?'
The children backed away, 'We didn't do anything' they cried.

But as they backed away they bumped into Daddy
And he landed in the pond with the goldfish splashing
But suddenly Mummy and the children started laughing
And spluttering and giggling until tears struck their eyes.

But Daddy didn't laugh because he was
Soaking!

Deanna Mills (7)
Girton Glebe Primary School, Cambridge

Weather

The sun was gleaming over the round Earth
It was as bright as a shining light in the day,
And it shone over the world as hot as an oven.

The rain splattered on the rocky, bouncy ground and
There were huge puddles in the black night,
The hard rain crunched like boulders falling on you.

The wind swirled in the air, it blew the trees' leaves off.
It madly made wrinkles in the water.
The leaves went round and round and trees swayed
In the breeze.

The lightning dazzled the ground and it made huge noises.
It blasted down from the silent sky, it slashed the floor.

Francis McGeoghegan (8)
Girton Glebe Primary School, Cambridge

The Four Seasons

Spring, summer, autumn and winter,
The four seasons of the year,
They bring joy, happiness, laughter and sadness,
You can never tell
When one is here
For they bring different things
Throughout the year.

Spring is a time for joy
It's when people play and dance around
Summer is a time for happiness
It's when hot weather arrives and makes
People sunbathe.

Autumn is a time for sadness
It's when the leaves go red and fall off the trees.
Winter is a time for laughter
It's when people have fun playing in the snow.

People love different times of the year
So say thank you to God that the four seasons
Are here.

Alexandra Riccio (10)
Girton Glebe Primary School, Cambridge

The Playground

The children play nearly every day with smiles on their faces.

The playground's always busy, with children having fun,
But I am one that crouches down sitting in a corner.

Some people say, 'Would you play?'
I jump up and say, 'Whoopee,' and go and join their game.
Their game is very jumpy, the grass is very lumpy
I said, 'Let's move,' so we jumped and we wiggled
And we jumped and we jiggled to the clean smooth grass.

The children play, nearly every day with smiles on their faces.
The sound of children playing makes my heart glow.

Alexandra Young (7)
Girton Glebe Primary School, Cambridge

The Seasons

Spring
Lambs are born
Buds appear on trees
New shoots spring up from the ground
A time to see a new beginning.
Summer
Flowers blooming,
The birds chirp merry tunes
Children have fun in the garden,
A time to enjoy and have lots of fun.
Autumn,
Days grow shorter
Flowers lose their petals
The trees have golden crinkly leaves,
Wonderful things still happen in autumn.
Winter,
All trees are bare,
We celebrate Christmas,
Blankets of snow cover the ground,
A great time to look back over the year.

Lucy Price (10)
Girton Glebe Primary School, Cambridge

The Pool

In the pool where the fish swim
I was looking for the shell
Where do I begin?
I was finding magic
When someone followed me
At the bottom of the sea.

Gracie Mills (7)
Girton Glebe Primary School, Cambridge

Lobster

In a restaurant one day,
I saw a lobster,
It was in a tank,
Its claws were tied,
Its head was bent.

A bloke,
Nodded his head at it,
As he talked to a waiter,
He continued to have a keen eye,
I saw it being taken away.

Later,
I heard a high pitched scream,
Knowingly,
Water welled from my eyes.

Was I the only one that cared?
That even knew,
That they had heard a creature,
That they had hurt me.

Peter Bock (10)
Girton Glebe Primary School, Cambridge

About Snow

Snow is sparkly
Snow is white
Snow shines.

I play in the snow all day
It's my favourite thing
I wish the snow would not go away.

Hannah Spraggs (7)
Girton Glebe Primary School, Cambridge

This Little Boy

This little boy
His name is Roy
And he is not coy at all
He had a mate
Who barely had a weight
Not that fat at all
He never knew his mumsie
He never knew pups
He had a fish
That lived in a dish
Now that is really odd
All he does is vacate
And exterminate
Probably cos he is eight
Wherever he goes
Cos that's how he rolls
He'll get those sweets and then home
He runs around like a headless chicken
This little boy is very sad
But he stops himself being very mad.
What does he eat?
He only eats meat
He has no religion
He always makes the wrong decision.

Will Donaghy (10)
Girton Glebe Primary School, Cambridge

The Skull

Sometimes our playtimes were boring and dull
But not on the day some boys found a skull.
A real human skull found in long grass
Where a ball had been kicked through too wild a pass.

They couldn't believe it looked like a stone
Except it had teeth and was made out of bone.

Pearl Mkwananzi (9)
Girton Glebe Primary School, Cambridge

I Wanna Be A Vet

I wanna be a vet,
I wanna heal a pet,
I wanna be the biggest name yet.
I said yeah, yeah, yeah
I wanna be a vet.

I wanna be a doc,
I wanna wear a frock,
I wanna lock my surgery
With a big fat lock.
I said yeah, yeah, yeah
I wanna be a doc.

I wanna be a healer
With my bandages cleaner,
I wanna do an operation
That's faster and cheaper
I wanna say yeah, yeah, yeah
I wanna be a healer.

I wanna be a vet
I wanna be a vet
But I ain't got very far . . .
Yet . . .

Gregory Chalmers (9)
Girton Glebe Primary School, Cambridge

Get A Little Soap

Get a little soap
Hold it in a grip
Rub it in your hands
Until they slip, slip, slip
Don't forget the dirt
Don't forget the ink
Wash away the suds
It's in the sink, sink, sink.

Bjorn Mkwananzi (9)
Girton Glebe Primary School, Cambridge

Night

The moon is out shining on me, shining on the world
below it.

People below it walking softly but there is still a
slight tapping when the shoes hit the pavement.

Lights are being switched off and people are going
to sleep.

Owls are out hunting mice and their wings are
beating swiftly, silently.

They're flying over the countryside with beady eyes
getting food for their chicks.

Badgers are scurrying around looking for worms and
are getting into people's dustbins.

Foxes are prowling around farms and killing the
helpless hens and rabbits that they find.

It is a cool spring night but not a still one, as it may
seem in story books.

If only stories told the truth about what really
happens at night.

Ben Horner (10)
Girton Glebe Primary School, Cambridge

'Twas The Night Before Christmas

'Twas the night before Christmas
All the children were in their beds.
Santa's special treat to wake up all the sleepyheads.
In just a flash, Santa gave everyone some cash,
He gave it out to the poor and Santa
Waited one year more.

Alex Lee (10)
Girton Glebe Primary School, Cambridge

A Trail Of Feelings

A trail of feelings lead from fury,
Which bubbles like molten lava.
Destroying everything in its path,
Fear floods from it.

Fear comes from anger,
A consequence of it.
It grips like a prison guard,
Never letting go.

Along with these two omens of darkness,
A light shines through the black.
The one in everyone,
Joy and happiness.

A smile, a laugh,
Can charm more than scowls.
They spread more than fright or fury.
And can bring out the best in everyone.

Laura Conboy (10)
Girton Glebe Primary School, Cambridge

It's Winter

When the fire crackles
And the wind howls
Cold wind goes down your spine.
When the trees sway,
And the snow falls,
You know it's wintertime.

When night falls
And the stars shine
Darkness comes before your eyes.
When the leaves fail to cling on
And the plants shiver,
You know it's wintertime.

Isabelle Austin (10)
Girton Glebe Primary School, Cambridge

Last Friday

Last Friday we all went away,
To stay in a cottage for a day.
We didn't have time to stop and stare,
We did all kinds of things while there.
The weather wasn't very kind to us,
Although we didn't make a fuss.
We didn't even see the sun,
But we had lots and lots of fun!
We played games, hide and seek,
We were tired and fell asleep
To dream that we would come again
To hope and hope it doesn't rain.
The time has come, we must go home
In the traffic (what a drone).
To our house our little nest
So to bed to get some rest.
To dream away, just to say
We will go there another day!

Jodie Langley (11)
Girton Glebe Primary School, Cambridge

I'm Writing Secret Words

I tread delicately on the freezing, barren landscape,
Spinning from line to line, flowing out sky-blue ink
That forms into my secret words.
I warm up my cold school page,
With neat letters.

My exclamation mark is a spout
I am never tired because my point
Is sharpened all the time.
I read what my lead has written
And the more I read,
The more it sounds like an old diary.

Who do you think I am?

Elizabeth Conboy (7)
Girton Glebe Primary School, Cambridge

Javert's Suicide

The cold strangles my heart and soul,
The stars no longer give me the guidance I need
They are as heartless as he is
And yet
Could I have been wrong all my life?
Could everything I have lived for be a lie?
We were sworn enemies
He could have been free
Just one single blow and I could have been another memory
His past life could have been forgotten
But he chose to kill me another way
He has destroyed everything I believed in
In one little act of mercy
Letting me go was worse than killing me
Because it killed my reason for living
I cannot live my life in debt to a convict
Especially not one I have been hunting down for ten long years
Ten long years wasted in just one second
I see no way out
The stars show nothing
They give no help
My hands let go of the bridge
The water covers me
This world is nothing now
We cannot exist in harmony
There is nothing left for me here
My time has ended.

Zoë Gault (10)
Girton Glebe Primary School, Cambridge

The Sea

The sea closed up in sunlight with only a ray of black.
All sorts of creatures lurk in the ocean.
Shipwrecks lie at the bottom.
Stingrays, whales and fish follow in the light of the sun.

Thomas Ridgeon (7)
Girton Glebe Primary School, Cambridge

Sweet Shop

After school me and my friends go to the sweet shop.
The sweet shop, the sweet shop.
We always have five pounds to spend.
At the sweet shop, the sweet shop.

I like the fizzy astro belts,
And the gummy sweets.
I always buy half a pound of Dolly Mix,
At the sweet shop, the sweet shop.

John likes the candy canes,
And the big chocolate bars.
He always buys a big bag of gum,
At the sweet shop, the sweet shop.

It's only when we've bought our booty,
Our mums come rushing in
And they confiscate our sweets galore
What a waste!

Ella Raff (10)
Girton Glebe Primary School, Cambridge

My Dog

I have a dog, who is black and white
He's a good friend both day and night.
Although for a walk he goes nearly mindless
All he really wants is food and kindness.

Before I go out to play in a rush
I have to remember to give him a brush
If not, the carpet will be covered in hairs
Already I see there is some on the stairs.

Sometimes in the house, Fidget and I will play a game
If something gets broke, he will get the blame.
When we have finished our fun, the ball he will keep
Go to his bed and fall fast asleep.

Josh Mansfield (9)
Girton Glebe Primary School, Cambridge

Tidal Wave

Today is your day of reckoning,
You who are weak will perish before me!
Those of you who are strong and true
Will be taken slower but be demolished too!

The storm's face disappeared but the eyes,
Black as death burned on, stabbing into the hearts
Of the mortal men assembled on the deck.
One jumped from the ship screaming with terror
Then fell slowly sinking like a wreck.

The ship moored on the island and the crew jumped off.
They set about crying warnings around the island.
One young fisherman saw a cottage on the mountainside,
He rapped on the door and was invited inside.

'Please sit down,' said the elderly man with a black glint in his eye,
The young man refused the offer and began his warning tale.
Whilst he was telling, the man asked with interest,
'What did you say boy?'
'The storm, it said killing all was its ploy.'

The old man sighed resigned to telling the island of its fate.
'The fact is,' he proceeded, 'it's not a storm it's a wave.
It's called the 'Demon Destroyer' and it leaves none alive,
Except two youngsters, to make the island survive.'

Five minutes later screams could be heard everywhere,
Death had opened its door and was inviting them in.
Buildings lay shattered, children were crying in flooded streets.
Then suddenly the waves came down and the children stopped
Crying as if given treats.

No sound. No whimpering. No crashing! The sound of *death!*

Then from the silence came a piercing cackle.
It was the old man! With two prisoners, the young fisherman and a girl.

Jonathan Shevlane (11)
Girton Glebe Primary School, Cambridge

What Excitement

What excitement today because it's my birthday,
I'll be seven and I'll get lots of lovely presents.

What excitement today because I'm going to France,
I will be having fabulous baguettes
And I'm going to Disneyland, Paris.

What excitement today because I'm going to my friend's house,
I will be playing hide-and-seek and we are playing It.

No excitement tonight because I'm going to my bed.

William Parker (8)
Girton Glebe Primary School, Cambridge

A Mess!

My dad's study is such a mess
When my mum says 'Clean up!' He says, 'Yes.'
But you can always bet
That for sure he'll forget
Till the clutter gets on to his desk.

Diana Nicholls (11)
Girton Glebe Primary School, Cambridge

The Tomb

The lost skeletons of dead people clattered
to the ground and echoed around the dark tomb.
The blood of dead people dripped onto the soggy
and wet stone
All you could hear were the rats munching their way
through the crunching bones.
The only light there was, was the sunbeam drifting
into the tomb.

Mikey Raff (7)
Girton Glebe Primary School, Cambridge

The Eagle And The Prey

He circles his prey,
Swooping down closer and closer.

The prey is trapped,
He has nowhere to go.

The eagle squeals
Swooping straight downwards
With his razor-sharp claws.

His prey dodges
And calls for help
But he has no luck.

His claws dug in
And took him up high.
Back to his home,
Up high in the trees,
He gives his prey to his family,
They rip it apart.

The eagle now goes in search of more prey,
Goes into the distance,
The mist,
Blood has been spilled that night.

The night was getting cold,
The eagle's family starved,
But the eagle did not return.

The eagle had been shot,
And in a farmer's field it lay,
Caught by the hunter,
Now the eagle knows what it is like
To be the prey.

Danny Pattern (11)
Girton Glebe Primary School, Cambridge

Got A Date

Dear diary, Saturday night . . .
Got a date with the birds
Got to look my best,
I want to be the prettiest.

Nibbling strawberries
Filling my tum,
Delicious berries everywhere
Beautiful accessories for my dress.

Oh what is the good of being a bug?
I feel as ugly as a slug.

I'm snug and tight,
In my thick cocoon.
I really hope
Spring comes soon.

I can feel the sun on my back,
Now my shell is beginning to crack.
Look at me, my wings are spread
A rainbow of colours from green to red.

Rachel Lee (10)
Girton Glebe Primary School, Cambridge

School

So boring and so dull,
How I wish I couldn't go
So very much indeed.

My brother he finds it OK
He's got a great teacher I have too.
I get rewards what about him?

Sometimes it makes me go green
Imagine that I would look strange.
But my favourite bit is when I am at home with
My family.

Natasha Phillips (10)
Girton Glebe Primary School, Cambridge

If Only

If only you could fly
like a pie in the sky.
If I could fly like a pie
I would fly high.

If only you could zoom
as fast as a tomb.
If I could zoom like a tomb
I would zoom, zoom, zoom.

If only you could jump
as high as a bump.
If I could jump like a bump
I would jump a bump.

If only you could glow
like a bow that says so.
If I could glow like a bow that says so
I would glow and say so.

If only you could float
like a goat in a coat.
If I could float like a goat in coat
I would float by a boat.

If you could do these things
You could perform for kings.

Simon Szymanski (10)
Girton Glebe Primary School, Cambridge

Sunflowers

My petals are as bright as the sun
They stand up to the sky,
The long, green, glimmering stalk I have
Stands straight and holds the rest of my body.
There is a bright light that shines from above
And twinkles on me.
I sparkle the most.

Emily Pattern (8)
Girton Glebe Primary School, Cambridge

Dogs

Poodles are curly, labradors are silky
German Shepherds are fluffy, greyhounds are not.
Tall Irish wolfhounds, short Westies.
Barking bulldogs, whining puppies.
Doberman Pinchers are thin, Jack Russells are chubby.
Pekinese are slow, collie dogs are speedy
Dalmations are spotty, shuffle board terriers are black
   All dogs are fun!

Lana D'Wilton (8)
Girton Glebe Primary School, Cambridge

The Easter Bunny

Here comes the Easter bunny
Come to fill your tummy
With chocolate eggs and honey
Foods that are so yummy.

In his little Easter basket
He carries chocolate eggs
Colourful, pretty, big and small,
The Easter bunny has them all.

Come again next year Easter bunny!

Luke Golding (9)
Girton Glebe Primary School, Cambridge

Snow

Snow is great you ride on a crate
Snow is white you get frostbite,
Snow is fun with the sun,
Snow is slushy and all mushy
Snow is great there is no break
Snow is cold like the North Pole
Snow is white you like a snow fight.

William Price (9)
Girton Glebe Primary School, Cambridge

Rose, Rose

Small petals fall from leaf to leaf
Autumn is coming!
But summer is here,
With the bright sun sparkling on rich earth.
My petals shine,
From the boiling sun.
It's true, it is.

My face is up high,
I'm as pretty as a princess.
It's true, it's true.

I wish I was as tall as a giraffe's neck
I shine up high with my beautiful petals.
I'm so pink and so pretty
It's true, it is.

Maddie Bean (7)
Girton Glebe Primary School, Cambridge

Midnight

No travellers go by,
Under the moonlight sky,
To live another day,
  The children start to play.
But then what hits them?
They don't know where to hide
As hideous creatures circle them with pride.
  Warlocks, corpses, vampires, hags
  Slink slyly to their side.
In seconds, minutes, hours, I guess
They leave only a blood-splattered dress.
  As two o'clock comes they all disappear
  They can't wait
  For their next victim
  To appear.

Anna Fleck (10)
Girton Glebe Primary School, Cambridge

Friends

Friends in the playground
Everyday
Friends in the street
Every week.
Coming and going
Even when it's snowing.
Playing fun and games
Even when it rains.
Relying on each other
To help one another.
As the day goes by
Round their house having fun.
Enjoying it in the sun.
Staying for tea
Is lots of fun
When they go on holiday
It's not so fun for me.
But when they come back
I sing *Hip Hip Hooray*
It's a happy day.

Katherine Burchell (9)
Girton Glebe Primary School, Cambridge

Midnight Feast!

At night I go downstairs,
To get some sweets for a midnight feast,
Sometimes we go in pairs,
'Cause I'm scared of the dark,
And there might be a shark.
I never get caught, cause I am the expert!
Then in the morning I get dressed, go down for breakfast,
But then there's my dad standing,
Ready for my daily spanking,
It's OK really, I feel just divine,
But there's something stinging on the bottom of my spine!

Cseperke Asztalos (10)
Girton Glebe Primary School, Cambridge

I Wanna Be A Gunner

I wanna be a Gunner
I wanna be my bruvver
I wanna go around on a big red runner
I said yeah, yeah, yeah
I wanna be a Gunner.

I wanna play for Arsenal
I wanna live in a castle
I wanna see my football wrapped up in a parcel
I said yeah, yeah, yeah,
I wanna play for Arsenal.

I wanna be a Gunner,
I wanna be a Gunner
But I ain't no stunner
I'm just a little dumber.

Toby Wright (9)
Girton Glebe Primary School, Cambridge

Candy

Sugar candy,
Fizzy candy,
Are delicious sweets.

Soft candy,
Hard candy,
Beat the rest.

Sweet candy,
Sour candy,
Together are yummy.

Sticky candy,
Smooth candy,
Attach to your mouth.

But the best of all is
Any candy!

Joshua Course (10)
Girton Glebe Primary School, Cambridge

Monkeys

Monkeys are as brown as a chocolate bar
They are very nutty
They eat bananas and act bananas
Monkeys are everywhere
I mean everywhere.

Conor O'Brien (7)
Girton Glebe Primary School, Cambridge

Thunder - Cinquain

Thunder,
Lions roaring
The tigers roar scares all
Some say it's when God gets angry,
Thunder!

Melissa Scott (9)
Girton Glebe Primary School, Cambridge

Gangsters

Knives in their shoes
Nasty and scary
And big hair
Gangsters.

Michael Holland (9)
Girton Glebe Primary School, Cambridge

Thunder - Cinquain

Thunder
Its roar is loud
It booms like a big drum
Some say it's God's temper tantrum
Thunder!

Francesco Beber Fraser (8)
Girton Glebe Primary School, Cambridge

I Wanna Be A Cat

I wanna be a cat,
I wanna be *the* cat,
I wanna miaow
Right now!
I said yeah, yeah, yeah
I wanna catch a rat!

I wanna be a cat
I wanna do that
I wanna eat a big fat rat,
I said yeah, yeah, yeah
I wanna have a rat!

I wanna be a cat
I wanna be *the* cat,
I wanna miaow
Right now!

David Wilson (9)
Girton Glebe Primary School, Cambridge

Tomb

Haunted and grey
Full of vicious spiders
Spirits rise from the dead
Echoes boom from the stone
Great silence erupts!

Stephen Smith (8)
Girton Glebe Primary School, Cambridge

Tall Castle

Tall castle
Crooked castle
Ragged castle
Ruined castle.

Joanna Perera (8)
Girton Glebe Primary School, Cambridge

Wonderful Dolphins!

A bottlenosed dolphin is a bottle-necked mammal
Its smooth skin shimmers as the sun gleams down
The calm sea glimmers
When the dark waves frown.

A dolphin is a steady ski
Skimming across the water
Her fin turns over and waves to me
And many fishermen have seen her!

Danielle Smith (8)
Girton Glebe Primary School, Cambridge

Snow

Snow is white,
Like doves at night,
Snow is bright,
Like angels in the night.
Winds whistle,
Like wolves at night,
Snow like thistles
Blown at night.

Rhea Andrews (9)
Girton Glebe Primary School, Cambridge

Snow Poem

Time to wrap up warm
The snow has come
And it's a mighty storm
'Don't go out there,' yelled my mum
'It's too cold
It will freeze your tum!'

Rebecca Shevlane (8)
Girton Glebe Primary School, Cambridge

I Wanna Play In Blue! (For Chelsea)

I wanna play in blue,
I wanna beat you,
I'm a football hero, all brand new,
I said yeah, yeah, yeah, I wanna play in blue.

I wanna be a hero,
I don't wanna be zero,
I wanna be the new Del Piero,
I said yeah, yeah, yeah, I wanna be a hero.

I wanna play in blue,
I wanna play in blue,
But . . .
I've only got a job in the local zoo!

Christopher Scott (8)
Girton Glebe Primary School, Cambridge

The Waking Of The Ghost

Still, dead
Starts to arise
Takes a fly from his church
Off to scare the boys and girls.

Nightmare.

Alice Duncan
Girton Glebe Primary School, Cambridge

Snow

Snow is slushy,
Gooey and mushy
Snow is white
Like roads at night
What a beautiful sight
Light night.

Jack Kempton (9)
Girton Glebe Primary School, Cambridge

Fairy Music

When the fiddlers play their tunes, you may sometimes hear
Very softly chiming in, magically clear.
Magically high and sweet, the tiny crystal notes
Of fairy voices bubbling free from tiny fairy throats.

When the birds at break of day chant their morning prayers,
Or on sunny afternoons pipe ecstatic airs,
Comes an added rush of sound to the silver din
Songs of fairy troubadours gaily joining in.

When athwart the drowsy fields summer twilight falls,
Through the tranquil air there float elfin madrigals, and in wild
November nights, on the winds astride,
Fairy hosts go rushing by, singing as they ride.
Every dream that mortals dream, sleeping or awake, every love!
Fragile hope - these the fairies take,
Delicately fashion them and give them back again
In tender, limpid melodies that charm the hearts of men.

Amanda Moller (10)
Girton Glebe Primary School, Cambridge

The Big Bang

In the beginning there was nothing
Then out of nowhere came something.
A king in all his glory he rose
And with him he brought his friends, family and foes,
Which all eventually began to dance in twos and threes.
His family became stars,
His friends planets
But his foes were not as just,
They sulked and fought
Until they were able to turn a planet to dust.
But still invisible to you or me,
Black holes will be the death of us
From the tiniest particle to the mightiest galaxy.

Luke Perera (10)
Girton Glebe Primary School, Cambridge

Crocodiles

C is for a crocodile, chomping on a bone,
R is for the roaring as he brings all his prey home.
O is for the octopus, he snaffled from a crate,
C is for the catfish, which suffered the same bad fate.
O is for a big fat ox, freshly killed today
D is for the doom, which meets all of his prey
I is for the icky goo, which drips from his claws
L is for the licking tongue, which hangs from his jaws.
E is for the eagle which he quickly killed today,
S o look out - it may be you -
   Next time you step on a log that's greeny-grey!

Vicky Chalmers (10)
Girton Glebe Primary School, Cambridge

Three Friends

We are three friends
Zoe, Hannah and me.
When they come over we have so much fun.
When they leave I want them to stay.
When they leave I say they'll come again.
So next time they come we'll have so much fun.

Victoria Nicholls (7)
Girton Glebe Primary School, Cambridge

The Life Of A Cat

Swish of tail,
Padding paws,
Gently flexing
Long sharp claws,
Catch a mouse and pad away,
That's the layout of a cat's day.

Georgina Emery (9)
Girton Glebe Primary School, Cambridge

Best Friends

You're my best friend
And always will be
We can play on the playground
Just you and me.

We never fall out
We'll be just fine
We can walk about
You'll always be mine.

Claire Sharp (9)
Girton Glebe Primary School, Cambridge

Rain

I come,
I drench,
I feed the land,
I bring joy,
I bring sadness,
I bring sorrow,
I bring pity,
But no one
Says
Thank you.

Ewan Wilson (10)
Girton Glebe Primary School, Cambridge

The Seasons

Winter is cold and I play inside
Summer is hot and I play outside
Autumn is cool and I play in the leaves
Spring is warm and I see flowers spring up
I like summer the best.

Charlie Dean (7)
Girton Glebe Primary School, Cambridge

The Old Tree

You were alive before I was
I took care of you, I watered you.
You grew and grew until you could grow no more,
You have lived for two hundred years.
I wish I was you, you are lucky I am not.
I am me, you are you.
I played under you since I was two.
Until I could play no more.
I climbed as high as you.
I jumped off of you.
I swung from your branches without a swing
I made a treehouse in your middle.
I picked your fruit from your twigs as birds laid their eggs.
But now they want to cut you down.
They will not cut you down.
You shall not fall to the ground, not while I live.
I shall fight for you, I shall die for you,
I want you to live and if I have to die, then so be it.

Meitar Blumenfeld (10)
Girton Glebe Primary School, Cambridge

Bucks Fizz

Bucks Fizz (my pony)
Is a characteristic girl.
She is very, very fizzy,
And is the colour of pearl.

Bucks Fizz, as I call her,
My best friend, I would say.
For I tell her all of my troubles,
So that they go away.

She is what I would call a furry friend,
She is lazy, not at all busy.
I will love her for ever and ever,
That darling, pony, Fizzy.

Sabina-Maria Zappia (10)
Gresham Village School, Norwich

Tess

I have a dog who is a Border collie
And she is so gentle like a china dolly.

She is just like a little sweetheart
And hates The Simpsons especially Bart.

She is black and white
And would never bite.

She's got really beady eyes
And she has never met any guys.

When we take her on a walk she hates the lead,
Her little tag on her collar is like a glistening bead.

I love her to bits and she is my very best mate,
She is very clever and can open a gate.

Natalie Kinsley (10)
Gresham Village School, Norwich

Orange

Orange is the fruit
That melts in your mouth!

Orange is the sun
That brightens up the world!

Orange is the flower
That blooms every summer!

Orange is the fire,
That gives you warmth and glow!

Orange is the sand
That sinks beneath your feet!

Orange is the cheese
That people like to eat!

Orange is the world
Where lots of people meet!

Holly Wright (11)
Gresham Village School, Norwich

I Wonder What's In The Sky

(Thoughts of a small girl as she goes through her day)

I wonder what's in the sky when I wake up,
My mum says there are clouds in the sky far, far above.
I wonder what's in the sky while I eat breakfast,
My big brother says there are birds in the sky that can fly.
I wonder what's in the sky on my way to school,
My friend says there is a sun in the sky that shines.
I wonder what's in the sky at lunchtime while I eat.
My teacher says there's a moon in the sky at night.
I wonder what's in the sky at bath time,
My little duck says there are stars in the sky.
I wonder what's in the sky at bedtime.
My dad says God's in the sky, way, way up high.
After that I don't wonder any more because
I'm fast asleep! Shh!

Jennifer Holt (11)
Gresham Village School, Norwich

Ice Cream

I like ice cream
With everything in the world
I like it with roast
And I like it on toast
I like it with mousse
And I like it with goose
I like it with honey
And I like it with bunnies
I like it with coffee
And I like it with toffee
But best of all I like it with . . .

To be continued . . .

Charlie Fiddian (10)
Gresham Village School, Norwich

I Want

I want a swimming pool
But it would be too big for the garden.
I want to burp at the table,
But I always have to say pardon.

I also want a milkshake maker
So I can pour it all over the baker!

'We can't afford it,' says my mummy
So I just storm off and think she's crummy!

Joanna Annison (10)
Gresham Village School, Norwich

Black

On the way here, on the way there
Black is not rare
On the way up, on the way down
Touch *black* if you dare
Gloomy room
On the way to *doom*
Everything goes *black.*

Jessie Kellock (10)
Gresham Village School, Norwich

Red

I go this colour when I am embarrassed,
It mixes into the swirls in your dreams,
It resembles a big volcano, just about to erupt.
You see it when you are really angry or really jealous,
You feel it in the summer, in the scorching heat
And you sense it on the verge of danger.

Theo Young (10)
Gresham Village School, Norwich

Yellow

Yellow reminds me of Easter chicks
hatching in the spring.

It reminds me of the golden bright sun
acting like a king.

It reminds me of cheerful people always
happy to sing.

Yellow is lively, warm and filled with happiness.

Yellow, yellow, yellow, oh the joy you bring.

Lucy Hardy (11)
Gresham Village School, Norwich

If, If, If, If . . .

If I had a pony I would ride it every day,
If I had a car, I would drive everywhere.
If I won the lottery I would be a millionaire,
If I owned a wood I would get a grizzly bear.
        If, if, if, if, if!

Florence Blyth (10)
Gresham Village School, Norwich

Meat

Meat on my plate,
It's heavy like a crate,
The meat on the plate,
Staring at his mate.
Eat boy eat,
But I don't like that meat.

Jonathan Hayman (10)
Gresham Village School, Norwich

Funny Poem

Santa is a winner
He puts spice on his dinner
He flies into a Christmas tree
And all the presents are just for me!

Rudolph's toes are smaller
Than his nose
It's so red.

Elves are flash
As fast as a dash
They end up in a crash
Smash, smash, smash.

Mrs Santa's dress
Is as green as cress
She makes cakes
As small as a flake.

Chris Reed (8)
Lee Chapel Primary School, Basildon

A Fun Day At Thorpe Park

Rushing through the gates
With my ticket in my hand
Running to the playground
And playing in the sand.

Going on the water log
Queuing up in cages
Finally getting on the ride
Then I said, 'It was worth queuing up for ages!'

Then going on the roller coaster
It goes as fast as a car
I was screaming and yelling
And as we went past I rattled the bar.

Rebecca Smith (8)
Lee Chapel Primary School, Basildon

My Dog

My dog's mad
He sleeps upside down with his legs in the air
He chews his towel everytime
He bites ankles when I'm in the garden
He tears around the garden like a thing possessed.
          It's my dog.

When my mum is in the garden
He's as noisy as can be
He is as dark as a tree
And as soft as silk
          It's my dog.

I love my dog
He is the best dog ever
I will never forget my dog
But he is so cheeky.

Timothy Churchill (8)
Lee Chapel Primary School, Basildon

Protect The Wildlife

As I'm walking through the wild jungle
And stepping on the squelchy mud
Suddenly I hear something!
Whimpering from the animals hunted
For fun.
Animals' tears and fears.
While hunters walk away
Cheers and happiness and loudness
As the blood of a poor animal is still pouring.
Screams, yells, blood, whimpers in pain.
Let's stop it please
Give an animal a good life
It should be the end of hunters
It could be the end of hunters for you and me.

Misha Towler (8)
Lee Chapel Primary School, Basildon

Flowers

The smell and the sight were intoxicating
I could see the stunning flowers around
In the breeze I saw them dancing
What a brilliant sight to see.

Walking through the gardens
I see such exciting things
I can see something bright again
Oh look it's a wonderful rose.

What more would I like to see here?
There are many flowers in the world
I would pick one of each, if I could
To look at every day.

I sit here looking happy
With all my flowers here
What more would you want in my garden?
Nothing, such brightness all year.

Taylor O'Neill (8)
Lee Chapel Primary School, Basildon

Snow

Everyday it snows
And everybody knows
The sun comes out and melts it away
And it really, really spoils the day.
I go out into the snow, I see a big footstep.
I hear little birds singing in the tree.
It's lovely in the sunset.
I see the sun glistening in the air
It's lovely as a fair.
I love the snow
Everyday I go outside
My mum comes out and says, 'Hello.'
And that is the end of the beautiful day.

Brooke Saunders (8)
Lee Chapel Primary School, Basildon

The Highwayman

Riding on, on, on,
His French cocked-hat a glimmer,
His rapier a shine,
His lace a flash,
His pistol butts a deathly black.
He rode trotting, trotting, trotting,
Along the stream of silver, along the mauve hills.
Over the plains, the hills, the mountains
Galloping, galloping, galloping.
Through the town along, along, along.
He rode up to the inn,
He knocked, knocked and knocked
It creaked open, slowly, slowly, slowly,
But it wasn't his girl.
All that was heard was a single musket shot
And silence.

Christopher Johnson (10)
Lee Chapel Primary School, Basildon

Summer

Early morning sunshine everywhere
Flowers dancing in the air,
I run into the golden sun
Happy I gallop all around as a butterfly.

Summer breeze gently touches my face
Nature is having fun - it's a beautiful sight,
Grasshoppers making a noise - it comforts me
As I settle into my deckchair.

As it gets dark all the flowers dip their head
And go to sleep.
As the sun awakes all the flowers
Start to have fun again!

Lucie Frater (8)
Lee Chapel Primary School, Basildon

The Storm

Crash! I sat bolt upright
All the room around me was white
Crash! The TV had gone fuzzy
The aerial was blowing back and forth.

Boom! Lightning hit a tree,
The tree caught light,
And then it toppled down,
But it put up a terrible fight.

I could taste salt water in the air,
The smell of the seaside was everywhere.
The wind was roaring round and round
As lots of things came to ground.

Oh what a mighty storm,
It's times like this I'm glad I'm tucked up warm.

Robert Scowen (8)
Lee Chapel Primary School, Basildon

The Clown

A clown is very funny
When he jumps up like a cat
A clown is very crazy
And very, very fat.

A clown throws pies,
A clown juggles,
A clown is very silly
And keeps on tripping over.

A clown does nothing but eat,
And also drinks some beer,
He also kisses a bat
And also loves a hat.

Melih Manyera (8)
Lee Chapel Primary School, Basildon

A Fun Day Through Park

I charge along the gates with a ticket in my hand
I jump up and down like a cricket trapped on hard ground.
I jump into the queue and wait ages, it was like I was in cages.
Now I get to have my go.
I sit down and close my eyes.
I chew some chewing gum.
Now it's time to go, it goes very cautiously up and then . . .
It screams down!
My hair standing at the tip, my shoe was falling off.
I was now frightened to death.
As it goes down it is travelling
Like the speed of light.
It was unbelievable . . .
Then an amazing thing happened
We go into a tunnel
Machines come - attack us from everywhere
It was soon over.

Sohaib Ahmad (9)
Lee Chapel Primary School, Basildon

Footie

Balls flying through the air,
Knocking off people's hair.
It's a goal kick here,
Come on folks, drink some beer.
The second half gets underway,
Will you come and watch us play?
Owen shoots,
With his boots,
He scores again
But . . . he seems to be in quite a pain!
The game has finished now,
I must get home to play with my pal.

Sam Carmichael (9)
Lee Chapel Primary School, Basildon

Animals In The Wild

I'm walking through the jungle
As swiftly as a chimp
I'm looking up in the trees
I see orang-utans and gorillas
Swinging from tree to tree.

I'm going on Safari
In the African heat
I see a hungry lion
Looking for his prey.
He's a really hungry lion
He wants me to eat
Laughing as a hyena
As racy as a wildebeest
I like Africa don't you?

I'm swimming through the ocean
I see a great white shark.
With 3000 big teeth
Ripping through his prey
He's a really hungry monster
I hope he won't come my way!

Nathan Connor (9)
Lee Chapel Primary School, Basildon

From The Seat Of A Car

Rumble tumble things pass by,
Trees and a woman with an apple pie.
The rain came down and made me frown .
I have a rash from a crash.
I bashed and dashed and the window smashed!
Faster and faster we go round the corner -
I saw a rainbow.
We went past lakes we made earthquakes.
The day was bad and sad!

Jessica Moss (9)
Lee Chapel Primary School, Basildon

My Cat Boo

I have a fat cat,
Who sits on the mat,
She's big and round
And never makes a sound.

When I have something to eat,
She is always by my feet.
When I have some fish,
I give her some on her dish.

She likes to sleep in the sun,
It looks like she is having fun.
When she purrs
I stroke her fur.

I love my cat
Her name is Boo,
I know that she loves me too!

Hayley Chrystie (8)
Lee Chapel Primary School, Basildon

Cat

As spiteful as a lion
As fast as a train
As cheeky as a monkey
She hasn't got a brain
As sleepy as a sloth
As greedy as a dog
As happy as a bee
She thinks she's a log
As scary as a ghost
As fierce as a tiger
As bright as a person
But I think she's getting kinder.

Molly Dowling (9)
Lee Chapel Primary School, Basildon

Flowers

I love roses
Yellow as the sun
My eyes flow straight to them
Once your eyes catch the sight
It's impossible to drag your eyes away
I love daisies too
White as snow
I sends a shiver down my spine
On a fresh daisy it has pink splodges on the edge
I like the poppy most
As red as our school jumper
It reminds me most of school, working all day
I would like to wake up in a field of poppies
Flowers make the world a brighter place
With their sweet scent in the air.

Chloe Fowler (8)
Lee Chapel Primary School, Basildon

A Hot Day In Summer

The sun is beaming down on me
Giving me a tan
Sunbathing is so much fun
Summer is my favourite season.

Splashing water at one and other
Soaking all my body
Swimming is fun, so fun,
Especially in summer.

Sun looks so delightful
Yellow, orange and red
Beaming down on you
On a hot day.

Charlie Boshell (8)
Lee Chapel Primary School, Basildon

The Black Cat

The black cat's fur is battered and bruised
It gleams in the light of the moon
His sharp jagged claws sparkle
With red blood dripping to the ground.

The glistening creature prowls around in the dark
While the hammering rain soaks him through and through.
His yellow jewel-like eyes glare and he bares his teeth
At anyone who comes near,
And arches his back to let out a vicious hisssss . . .

The black cat moves around swiftly
But people get a glimpse of him here and there
The mysterious creature is only out at midnight
Because in the morning he's never there.

George Hunt (9)
Lee Chapel Primary School, Basildon

Creepy Cave

Staggering through the swerving cave
Gashes through my heart
Screaming coming through the walls
Water dripping heavily, I'm sure to say
Death death repeatedly
Mice scratching at the ground
Trying to escape this terrible place.

Spiders struggling down my neck
Snake wrapping around my leg
Shadows dancing on the walls
Trying to dodge the falling rocks
The cave will be collapsing soon
Got to get out and fast.

Kieran Eldridge (9)
Lee Chapel Primary School, Basildon

Snow

The snow
       whirls
          twirls

The snow is settling
Laying a white carpet over the icy path
          drip
             slip

The snow covers your house
As a white cloak closes you in
         glisten
           just listen.

Footsteps on the melting snow,
Shining like a diamond in a gold mine
        crunch
          scrunch.

Harry Gadlin (9)
Lee Chapel Primary School, Basildon

The Sun

The sun is a fire burning all the time.
It flames and smokes, heating up my thigh.
The sun is a fire with ashes leaping out
As if they were swimming through the sky.

The sun is a child all tucked up in bed
But when the moon disappears he gets back up again.
The sun is a child all happy and glad
But when it's time to hide away he settles down and cries.
The sun is a star glittering and gleaming brightly
As the moon sleeps away.
The sun is a star brightest of all
It's always on time, never late, gleaming all the way.

Peter Bines (9)
Lee Chapel Primary School, Basildon

Rain

Rain is the worst day of my life
Especially when I go to school
The rain comes gushing down on me
As if I've been splashed in a pool.

The rain comes gushing
Onto the ground
There's a lot of rain
Dripping from that door.

When I finish school
And it is still raining
I wish I could get a taxi
Hey isn't that my friend Maxi?

I go up to my friend Maxi's home
But his mum cannot take me
So I go, trying
Not to step on any puddles
And lean against the tree.

I finally reach home
And see my teddy Ted
I hug him and squeeze him
But my mum comes in and says,
'Go and water the flower beds!'

Lois Mensah-Afoakwah (8)
Lee Chapel Primary School, Basildon

Naughty Cats

My cat is fat and she acts like a rat,
My cat is fat and she sat on my mat,
My cat is poor and she can't open the door,
My cat is raw, and she don't follow the law,
My cat is sad and she's really, really bad,
My cat is mad and I'm very, very glad!

Apphia Williams (9)
Lee Chapel Primary School, Basildon

Rain War

Droplets like spears came charging down,
Cutting into the surface of the earth.
Puddles slurping up all it needs greedily,
With his beckoning tongue.
Fresh water daggers crept into my nostrils,
Stabbing and making my soft nose bloodshot,
Blocking my blood vessel's journey
Whipping wind combed sharply waking my face,
Feasting on my vulnerable skin.
I sucked in the clean air,
My nose twitched,
I could sense her war
Come to a halt and she died down,
And laid dead drops of water calm and still
Leaving me wet and empty.
Alone!

Aamna Khan (10)
Lee Chapel Primary School, Basildon

Swimming

Diving through the crystal water
Making a big splash
Going down the massive slide
And having a big crash.
Going underwater
Trying not to breathe
My eyes are stinging as hard as they can
Like really big bumblebees.
Going on the inflatable
Having a fun time
Lying on my belly
In all the slippery slime.

Devon Barr (9)
Lee Chapel Primary School, Basildon

Rainforest

Prickly trees waving their big, bold fingers frantically,
Bending branches swaying and dancing elegantly.
Long, luscious grass tickles my tingly toes,
Bright, beautiful flowers smell like perfume.
Whistling winds passing through my knotty hair making it
Stand on end,
An exciting shiver runs down my bending spine.

Strings of grass sways longingly,
A bitter damp taste of the misty air down my dry throat.
Rain comes joyfully dancing down licking the tree tops,
Trickling down my excited face.
Whipping winds forcing me further away from the fascinating
rainforest.

Looking over my shoulder
As I walk away
Remembering . . .

Leanne Warren (10)
Lee Chapel Primary School, Basildon

Winter

In the winter the houses are like cakes
The branches of the trees are like witches fingers
All the flowers have gone away
And everywhere is icy.

I love to have snowball fights
And build snowmen
And I also love to make snow angels
And write my name in the snow.

At last I go home
It is warmer inside
Then the snow melts away
To come again next winter.

George Case (8)
Lee Chapel Primary School, Basildon

Mary

We have a leader at Cubs
Her name is Mary,
But we also call her Rak Sha
She is as kind as a fairy.

Mary cooks us food at camps
She gives us second helpings,
Sometimes she calls us little scamps
There would be no Cubs without Mary.

She jokes about
Laughs and shouts,
Takes our subs
And counts them up.

She rushes about
And she sorts stuff out
But always finds time
To sit down and tell a gory horror story!

I wrote this poem
Because you're ill
I hope you can read this
And it cheers you up
Hope you get better soon
And come back to Cubs.

James Genes (9)
Lee Chapel Primary School, Basildon

Sun

When there is no sun at all
I seem to be really tall
I miss the yellow sun in the sky
It seems to make me want to cry
People say it's like a light
But I think it's like a ball of fire.

Steven Le Count (8)
Lee Chapel Primary School, Basildon

Summer

Hooray, summer is here again!
Dancing flowers, gently sway
Exotic colours like a painting
Lovely smells from the wonderful roses
Newborn buds start to grow
Willow trees sway in the warm breeze
Giving shelter to the little plants below
Apples say goodbye to the branches
Leaves twirl off and find a new home
Birds singing sweetly in the sunshine
Swooping blue birds fly in the heat
Sitting under the shady trees
Lazing in the blazing sun
Butterflies flutter from blade to blade
Ladybirds rest on the cool leaves
Buzzing bumblebees collecting nectar
Spindly grasshoppers in disguise
Squirming worms burrow in the cool mud
The end of the day is drawing near
The sun is sinking in the sky
The last colours are fading away
One more glimpse and . . . *gone.*

Courtney Wardell (8)
Lee Chapel Primary School, Basildon

Rats

They're as hungry as a tidal wave
They eat and sleep all day
They nip you when you're near them
I'm positive of that!

I have to feed them every day
But they hardly ever move
And when I looked up on them
They weren't in the mood.

Emma Beard (8)
Lee Chapel Primary School, Basildon

My Friend

My name is Ebony Lynn
My best friend's name is Danai Kim.
We like mucking about
And we like going out
To have fun with other friends.

My best friend's name is Rhiannon Lewis
She likes wearing clothes that are kind of bluish!
We like being funny
We like finding money
And sharing with other friends.

My best friend's name is Hannah Bull,
She is very small and I'm very tall,
We like playing together
Whatever the weather
To cheer up other friends.

My best friend's name is Rosie Bird,
She always tells me what she heard
She is my Brownie buddy
And never gets muddy
And loves my other friends.

Ebony Lynn (8)
Lee Chapel Primary School, Basildon

Autumn

Walking through the shrivelled, crisp leaves,
The ground is like a moving carpet,
With the gusty wind whistling past me,
The trees are waving,
Shedding their leaves,
Making shadows all around,
The colours are golden, brown and red,
The season's changing,
Autumn is on its way.

Alexander Bird (9)
Lee Chapel Primary School, Basildon

Moonlight

The silver coat of the moon gleamed high up in the sky
Silence was all around - so silent it was deafening.
Nothing but my black shadow was to be seen
The moon lit up the dark night
As it shone upon the city of people
Sleeping unaware.

I heard the hoot of the owl
As I reached out for the silvery tree
The silver paws of the dog poked out of his warm, homely kennel
A rustle, as I turned round the moon winked at me.

There I saw a fox, a silver one, rummaging through the bins
He looked up at me
The moon reflected his silvery eyes, sparkling
I blinked
He was gone.

Megan Williams (10)
Lee Chapel Primary School, Basildon

A River

A trickle from the river
In a cornfield
The widest you've ever seen
Trickling even further.
It's getting wider
Getting like a disco ball
A pretty scene to see
Rushing ever downwards.

It's rushing to the sea's mouth
Sparkling like road
A wild scene to see
Pretty as a glittering ocean.

Mitchell Wilk (9)
Lee Chapel Primary School, Basildon

Winter

The sparkling snowflakes fall on the ground
Soft and silent without any sound
I'm in a sea, full of white snow
Sparkling, glistening everywhere I go.

The wind is calm
The trees are still
Look there's a robin perched upon my window sill.

As I walk snow crunches beneath my feet
My cheeks are rosy red and my eyes begin to weep.
The snow is going and melting away
But it doesn't matter
I'll see it again another day.

Zahraa Ejaz (8)
Lee Chapel Primary School, Basildon

The Seaside

Running through the beach with the sun's haze
Waves eating the sand with salt water
Toes getting wet from the golden sand
Shells from the sea with the sound from the sea inside
There's strange noises in the cave close by.

The waves waving hello
The people swimming in the sea
The sand boiling under your feet
The ice creams melting from their hands.

The water rushing away
The people have gone and a deep dark night begins
Now it is time for me to go with the water bright
Now everything's gone, but just the moon and the bright sea.

Michael Lynch (8)
Lee Chapel Primary School, Basildon

Snow

The snow
        drifts
           Lifts
hitting you like a tonne of bricks
as the wind
      twirls
      swirls
blowing you across the white carpet
and white crumbled trees
      smash
         bash
the trees fall down from the power of the furious storm
While children
      cry
        and say why
It calmed, it was over
The snow was like a soft teddy bear tickling my skin
                tickle
                    giggle.

Craig Hookings (9)
Lee Chapel Primary School, Basildon

Funny Things

Mrs Santa wears a lovely dress
The colour is like fresh cress.
My daddy is a sailor
And I'm getting paler.
I'm feeling cool
Now I'm in my pool.
On Monday I get up late
But I have to go to school at eight.
I see an open drawer
The person who wrote this poem is
A joker I hope.

Adam Summerfield (8)
Lee Chapel Primary School, Basildon

Leisure

'What life this, if full of care
We have no time to stand and stare.'
No time to sit and watch the swans,
Flutter their wings where the swan belongs,
No time to climb the willow trees,
And wander around staring at leaves.
No time to stare at nature's world,
When the stars up high twirled and swirled.
'A poor life this, if full of care,
We have no time to stand and stare.'

Megan Cleverley (9)
Lee Chapel Primary School, Basildon

At The Funfair

I was on a roller coaster going up and down,
Then I played jokes with a funny clown,
I went on the see-saw it was so much fun,
After I went on the shooting stall, knocking the tins
                                    down with a gun.
I then went on a water ride and got soaking wet,
After, I won a cuddly teddy bear and I took him home
                                    as my pet.

Lauren Borley (8)
Lee Chapel Primary School, Basildon

Autumn

A mber and brown are the colours of the leaves
U nder the trees leaves have fallen
T rees are bare just the bark to keep them warm
U mbrellas are needed for the rain
M uddy puddles for jumping in
N ights are cold and very dark.

Amber Thurlow (8)
Lee Chapel Primary School, Basildon

Rain

Calmly rain spits against my cold, numb face,
Raindrops melt on my warm, red tongue,
Hailstones knock viciously on my white windowpane,
Overhead, thunder rumbles loud and clear,
Lightning flashes brightly from above.

Finally the lightning switches off,
Thunder at last has eaten, it's full,
Hailstones leave the path unwelcomed,
Raindrops then evaporate,
The rain is being kind,
And the cold face mask is removed!

Zoë Hales (11)
Lee Chapel Primary School, Basildon

Playing In The Snow

Building a snowman it's lots of fun
Got to find my lonely Mum
My cat jumped on to the frozen lake
Then I died, for goodness sake!
Snowflakes glistening in the air,
Some are not landing, I don't care!
My snowman's died now from the sun
Bye-bye snow and everything, I had fun.

Joe Ludlow (8)
Lee Chapel Primary School, Basildon

What A Girl Wants

A girl needs friends that will cheer her up
When she's feeling down or fed up.
A girl needs mates just like you
But when you're small you make them up too!

Amy Cantwell (8)
Lee Chapel Primary School, Basildon

Twinkle Flakes

The snow
     twinkle
        sprinkle
out from the pale blue sky
as they drop
     curl
       swirl
They make a silky white carpet
as they land on the glistening green grass
              crunches
                scrunches

As people tread softly on them
all the remainders
       fly
      cry
until next year.

Heather Springer (10)
Lee Chapel Primary School, Basildon

A Night In The Woods

Alone in the cloudy woods late at night
Wolves howling continuously in the misty moonlit sky,
And echoes travel swiftly through the empty light.
Dark, long beckoning arms of shadowy trees,
Welcome you into a new frightful world
Their chunky shadowed bark smells slightly fresh.
I feel as cold as ice as shivers run down my startled spine,
Whipping wind hits my white shocked face,
And wet soggy grass tickles my bristling legs.
A slithery, squelchy leaf slips through my sweaty hand
As the coldness of the fresh air bites my rough tongue.
Whilst I tread alone in the woods,
On a cloudy night.

Charlotte Woods (10)
Lee Chapel Primary School, Basildon

Autumn

Autumn leaves sprinting around
Autumn leaves are all around
Leaves are blowing
Autumn is coming
Leaves are free all around
Trees are bare not wanting their leaves
To be on the ground
Trees are cold
Bushes are bold
We are warm
Bushes are cold by the time of dawn.

Gregg Mint (9)
Lee Chapel Primary School, Basildon

Four Tiny Kittens

Four tiny kittens climbing up a tree,
One fell and then there were three.
Three naughty kittens playing with the glue,
One got stuck and then there were two.
Two lazy kittens eating a bun,
One made lots of crumbs and then there was one.
One giggling kitten did all the housework
A broom fell on top of it and then there were none!

Mariam Khan (9)
Lee Chapel Primary School, Basildon

Lee Chapel Teachers

S cary teachers
C ool teachers
H elpful teachers
O ld teachers
'O rrible teachers
L ovely teachers.

Arron Armiger (9)
Lee Chapel Primary School, Basildon

A Snow Poem

Snow is soft
Snow is glistening
I love throwing it at my sisters
Throwing it at my mummy's house
Is so fun all day long
Riding in a sledge
And having fun
Snow is soft
Snow is glistening.

Molly Mackay (7)
Lee Chapel Primary School, Basildon

Animals

A ntelopes run gracefully
N ewts are very colourful
I guanas are very scaly
M osquitoes hurt me when I'm asleep
A nts scurry along the ground
L eopards are very, very spotty
S nakes, so slowly do they creep

Animals are wonderful in every way.

Rebecca Lewis (8)
Lee Chapel Primary School, Basildon

Material

A chair is hard
My bed is soft
My books are bendy
And so are my socks.
In a loft there was my sock
In my sock there was my foot.

Jodi O'Sullivan (8)
Lee Chapel Primary School, Basildon

Alligators Fishing

A lligators are sunny when they sleep
L ying on the river bank
L azing in the sun
I love alligators when they sleep
G iggling away when they're awake
A rguing over fish
T earing through the water
O ut and in the waterfall
R oaring very loud
S melly big animals

F ishing in the water
I love alligators when they sleep
S hh alligator is asleep
H itting each other
I love alligators when they sleep
N ibbling on food
G iggling away when they're awake.

Madeline Turner (8)
Lee Chapel Primary School, Basildon

Summer

When I went on holiday
In the nice hot sun,
I thought I saw Mum
Eating a hot cross bun.
Miaow, miaow, ouch, ouch
There's my cat on the sunbed.
Splish-sposh, spish-sposh
I dived in and bashed my head.
Oh my gosh is that the time?
I have to go straight home.
I have to go and sleep in my bed
If I don't my mum would have known.

Abbi Potts (8)
Lee Chapel Primary School, Basildon

The Polar Bear

When I was asleep in the bed
I saw something scratching his head
I touched his belly so warm and soft
I fell on him like a moth
I couldn't believe my eyes
It was a big surprise
I pushed him in the bed
And nearly bumped my head.

Jacey Ritchie (8)
Lee Chapel Primary School, Basildon

A Sea Poem

The waves go whoosh
The seagulls squawk
The boat needs a push
The sun shines bright on me while I sunbathe
The sea waves crash against the sand
People build sandcastles.

Becca Ingledew (8)
Lee Chapel Primary School, Basildon

A Poem

A cowboy fires an arrow
A fireman squirts out water
A teddy is nice, soft and warm
A gun is dangerous and powerful
Gunpowder blows up it can kill someone.
Boys are playful, a snake is scaly.
Mums and dads are nice to you
They let you have sweets.

Morgan Sprules (7)
Lee Chapel Primary School, Basildon

The Storm

The storm begins again
           bashing
           crashing
through the dusty clouds
as the wind
           curls
           twirls
wrapping its arms around the leafless trees
and the lightning
           dashes
           flashes
in the ink-black sky
while the storm
           rumbles
           bumbles
finding somewhere to hang its dark cloak.

Luke Townsend (9)
Lee Chapel Primary School, Basildon

Storm Poem

The wind blows up
           howling
             growling
Blowing through the trees
           snap
             crackle
The lightning flashes
           crash
             smash
The thunder sound
           boom
             bang.

Jamie Miln (9)
Lee Chapel Primary School, Basildon

Snow Storm

The snow
        swirls
           curls
In the dark blue sky,
as the light shines upon the snow
            crack
               smack
The lightning reaches the ground
with the snow as white as paper,
            ping
              pong
When the hailstones come crashing down
like frozen peas,
        hush
          shush.
Then silence falls upon the town
the snow storm has finished here today.

Amy McCormick (9)
Lee Chapel Primary School, Basildon

Winter Poem

Snow is like a white blanket
Covering the ground,
Freezing ice ball patterns
Spiral as they float down
Twinkling in the sunlight.

Frosty, slippery grass glistens
As spiderwebs get covered
With a silvery shine.
Has glitter been poured all around?
Icicles look like a bird's spiky claw
The shine of them sparkles in the sunlight.
They slowly melt, and they drip, drip, drip.

Hannah Jeffrey (10)
Lee Chapel Primary School, Basildon

The Storm

The storm begins again
                clashing
                and
                     bashing
against my windowpane
                pitter
                     patter
in the muddy puddles
                push
                     and pull
as the wind plays tug of war with
the trees.

William Sartain (9)
Lee Chapel Primary School, Basildon

The Big Storm

The storm begins again,
Splish, splosh to form a puddle,
Crash, bash, thunder
Rumbles across the gloomy sky,
Flash, bash, lightning zooms
With the speed of a car,
Moan, groan, the wind cries wildly.

Megan Mackay (10)
Lee Chapel Primary School, Basildon

Cloudy Day

One beautiful winter's day
The wonderful clouds appeared in the sky.
The colourful lights come sparkling down through the air
And the clouds glowed in the moonlight.

Clark Howe (8)
Lee Chapel Primary School, Basildon

A Medal Of Bravery

I know a man who has a medal
He keeps it safe in his drawer
He polishes it everyday
As he polishes it, his hurtful memory comes
                                    crawling back to him.
Remembering when he saved his family from a
                                    burning building,
The smoke was covering his mouth like a gag
Choking him to an evil death.
All he could remember was
When his children were huddling in the back of the room,
Gasping for a gulp of fresh air.
The flames this man could not bear,
Its angry mouth approaching
Chomping away at the children.
This memory will never go away
It will always be a place in his heart.

Lauren Claxton (10)
Lee Chapel Primary School, Basildon

Storm

The storm begins again
In the black sky
                splish
                                splash
The wind blowing and flowing
                                        moaning
                                        groaning
Out of the mad lips of the sky
The lightning flashes
                        crashes
Across the stormy moonlit night.

Rachel Brown (9)
Lee Chapel Primary School, Basildon

The Silver Birch Tree

Swaying in the misty sky
Sparkling like a star,
Soon its delicate branches
Will wind around the metal.
Dancing gracefully like Darcy Bussel
The bright green leaves swing round in a circle
And all around the beautiful bushes
Begin to rustle.
Extremely thin and tall is the stem
Moving, grooving to the beat
It is a remedy to cure all sad,
Never may the tree be bad.
Sparkling and glittering
As the sun beats down,
Too bright, the shining sun beams
And the special silver tree starts to wither.

Nicole Fowler (10)
Lee Chapel Primary School, Basildon

The Storm

The storm begins again
                drip
                    drop
Out of the ugly sky
Lightning
          clashes
            flashes
Across the gloomy sky
Rain tumbles, jumbles down my windowpane
                          sliding
                            gliding
Down the blank face of glass.

Amiee Townsend (9)
Lee Chapel Primary School, Basildon

Winter

Snowflakes tumble falling down,
Quickly settling on the ground
All the houses aglow with lights
Shining brightly, through the night
People rolling balls of snow
Making snowmen as they go
Santa Claus passing by
Quickly through the clear night sky
Piles of presents under the tree
Children's faces shine with glee.

Billie-May Colverson (11)
Lee Chapel Primary School, Basildon

The Pretty Red Rosie

The pretty red rosie
With another posie
If you touch her with your finger
You end up with a thorn in your finger!
She likes to be picked,
But in a few months
She'll fall forward
Flat on her face.

Alexandra Esme Knox (8)
Lee Chapel Primary School, Basildon

Autumn

A utumn is a peaceful time when it is sunny but cold
U mbrellas should be up when it is raining
T rees drop leaves and let them turn gold
U nbeaten by the wind, wet and shivering
M agpies fluttering all around me
N oises from the bird, amazing.

Michael Bird (7)
Lee Chapel Primary School, Basildon

I've Shrunk

Somehow I became an inch tall
I hid from some kids playing baseball
I got stuck on second base
I got into a cat chase
I got picked up by bees
I got stuck in the trees.

I went inside
I started to grow wide
I started to grow tall
I was back to normal.

Natalie Reynolds (10)
Lee Chapel Primary School, Basildon

Cat In The Snow

The glittering snow falls down from the sky
And sparkles in the moonlight.
It covers the grass like a giant's blanket.
The cat goes out on tip toe
He leaves his paw prints in the snow.
His tail starts to freeze as he plays in the snow.
He runs home and curls up by the fire.

Nicholas Fulton (9)
Lee Chapel Primary School, Basildon

Storm

Hailstones are ferocious giants destroying the town
The normal rain is an army throwing spears of water from the clouds,
The thunder is an angry child slamming the door on his mum
The lightning is a wizard in rage blocking out the sun.

Jamie Robertson (9)
Lee Chapel Primary School, Basildon

Leisure

'What life this, if full of care
We have no time to stand and stare.'

No time to hear the rustling trees,
As beneath them flows by the breeze.

No time to gaze into the sky,
As the blue birds pass you swiftly by.

No time to smell the lovely air
So that is why we have to care.

No time to feel the prickly grass
As helpless animals scurry past.

No time to taste the willow tree,
As nature itself is life's key.

'A poor life this, if full of care
We have no time to stand and stare.'

Kirsty Wood (10)
Lee Chapel Primary School, Basildon

Sun Rain Snow

Look out here comes the sun
Let's go out and have some fun
Quick put on some suntan lotion
Make it runny like a potion
Then it turns back to rain
I know it's come back again
It has become danger class
Parents telling children 'It will pass.'
Great it's going to snow,
Like arrows shooting from a bow.
Here comes a plough
Ploughing fields, cattle and cow.

Connor Randall (11)
Lee Chapel Primary School, Basildon

The Sea

The rappady monster
Clashes and bashes
The waving sea
Smashes and crashes.
The blue carpet is soaking the sand
Upon my feet,
Moving and rushing
To the beat.
The rhythm is swaying from side to side
And now it gives way for the seagulls to glide.
Slower and slower
Away from the groove
But soon another day
It will begin to move.

Kelly Burdett (10)
Lee Chapel Primary School, Basildon

The Haunted House

A scary bantree house
Which was the size of a lighthouse
Has lots of ghosts
That pretend to be hosts.

The stairs are always creaking
And the ceiling's always leaking
The house shakes
As the zombies bake cakes.

Skeletons can be mad
Happy or sad
And I should know
Because I live there.

Daniel Hawkins (10)
Lee Chapel Primary School, Basildon

Leisure

'What life this, if full of care
we have no time to stand and stare?'

No time to stand and watch trees grow
While up on a branch there sits a crow.

No time to see the birds flutter by
While blackbirds perch and peck some pie.

No time to play with your ball
While your mother sits in the cold swimming pool.

No time to stand and wave goodbye
Because you'll be back to say, 'Hi.'

No time to wait and watch things grow
While your sister does a little red bow.

'A poor life this, if full of care
we have no time to stand and stare?'

Katie Bird (10)
Lee Chapel Primary School, Basildon

The Highwayman

As he trotted on and on through the dusty night,
His stolen money in his pocket glistening bright
His brown long boots up to his knee
Silently taking money from you and me.
His black mask covering his face
And under his chin lace.
All his riches everywhere
He doesn't think, he doesn't care.
As he carries on through the night,
He waits for the morning bright.
He trots up to the inn door
On top of the silent moor.

Abbie Fry (10)
Lee Chapel Primary School, Basildon

The Storm

A clap of thunder shook the town
Lightning scorching the burnt, black sky
Thunder rumbling like a box of bones
A dagger of lightning stabbing the ground.
Rain thudding like a hammer on wood
Hailstones banging on the roof
The grey, grim sky turning black as coal
As the terrible storm moves on.
The sky splits in half
And lets a knife strike the ground
Sheets of shock cover the sky
Claps of thunder shaking the world
Finally the storm calms down
And only a puff of wind is heard
Rattling doors and windows gently
But soon only a light breath of wind.

Beth Burnet (10)
Lee Chapel Primary School, Basildon

Flower

The flower is an elegant dove
swaying from side to side
It is as soft as a ribbon of silk
and your hand would just glide.

The flower is a smiling face
never ever sad
It is always good and does as it is told
And never ever bad.

The flower is a dancer,
Like a very funny friend
it would dance all year round,
and never end.

Alice Bannon (9)
Lee Chapel Primary School, Basildon

Theme Park!

I walk through the gate
My body full with excitement
The children on the carousel
Their smiles filled with delightment!

> I can't decide what ride to go on
> They're all so big and new
> I can't take my time on them
> As there are definitely more than a few!

I go on all the huge rides
Screaming all the way
Upside down and loop-the-loop
It's turning out to be a great day!

> Now it's time to go home
> I was having so much fun
> Missing all the rides already
> But the adventure is done!

Christie Lee (10)
Lee Chapel Primary School, Basildon

Fire

Fire is like a raging rhino ready to rampage
through a China shop.
It is like a demolition site ready to blow.
Fire is like hate ready to overwhelm you
It is like a devil's eye watching your every step.

Fire is like a warning howling run
It is like the world of men coming to an end.
Fire has no end and what a sight if it could blend.

Fire is the sun as we know it
And we are the main course for it to devour.

Thomas Bakasa (9)
Lee Chapel Primary School, Basildon

I Know A Man

I know a man who has a medal, he keeps it in his drawer.
And every night he looks at it to remind him of his bravery
in the war.
He polishes it. He polishes it, and as he does this
He remembers, remembers, remembers.
And as he does this he remembers his bravery in the war.
I know a man who has a medal, not much to me and you.
But it means the world to him for his bravery in the war.
He remembers how he fought for freedom,
How he fought with all his might
And how his friends sacrificed their lives for others.
It may not be much to me and you,
But it means the world to him.
It was a long time ago, but never forgotten,
Because he won it for his bravery in the war.

Marina Mensah-Afoakwah (10)
Lee Chapel Primary School, Basildon

Blizzard

The blizzard breaks and creates
While all the cars get drifted, lifted
As the old man sleeps, beeps
All night long.

The blizzard roars and claws,
While all the dogs scream, dream,
As the poor beg for a leg,
All night long.

The blizzard jumps makes lumps
While all the horses run for their mums,
As the women drink wine so fine,
All night long.

Michael Christian (10)
Lee Chapel Primary School, Basildon

Medal

I know a man who's got a medal,
He keeps it in a drawer,
He polishes it and polishes it.
While polishing he remembers,
How he survived, how he survived,
How D-Day went,
How he destroyed a gun tower,
How he rescued two injured, stranded Privates,
The medal is small and coloured brown,
Nothing much - but when he sees it
It's a mirror into the past, the horrible past,
How he was frightened,
Pinned to his chest, he remembers.
How the bullets flew by,
Saved by God,
As he clinches it, a tear rolls down his face,
Then he remembers, he remembers.

Reece Hendy (10)
Lee Chapel Primary School, Basildon

Six Different Ways To Look At The Sun, Snow And Storms

The sun is a big friendly giant,
That smiles all the time,
He gives you warmth and love.

The snow is icing sugar being sprinkled
It's a snow globe scene
It's fluffy white cotton wool.

A storm is a child's stomach that's rumbling furiously,
An infuriated ogre taking it out on us,
Someone who just stubbed their toe.

Amy Prankard (10)
Lee Chapel Primary School, Basildon

The Tiger!

As I stand and watch this magnificent beast
He slowly staggers onto his four paws
Longing for his freedom
He stares at me with his big red sapphire eyes
Waiting . . .

Closer and closer he comes nearer,
I can hear his heart pounding wildly.
I can feel his warm dry breath as I put my trembling
Fingers further in.

We can smell fresh green grass
And the bark from the trees.
That's where he should be, in the jungle roaming free.
With other magnificent beasts just like him
But he's roaming around in a cold and lonely cage.

Whitney Billett (10)
Lee Chapel Primary School, Basildon

Leisure

'What life this, if full of care
we have no time to stand and stare?'
No time to watch the birds soar by,
making movements in the sky.
No time to look at nature's brook
gently running through the trees.
No time to look at nature's world,
when running water swirled and swirled.
No time to see the squirrels dart around
barely touching the bushy ground.
No time to stay with family
too busy buzzing like a bee.
'A poor life this, if full of care,
we have no time to stand and stare?'

Sam Spriggs (10)
Lee Chapel Primary School, Basildon

Tiger

His fur as golden as the sun
With eyes as sharp as knives
His fur as soft as a feather bed
Breath as cold as ice.

His lazy lounging tail
Sweeps the forest floor
Creating a mystical mist
Around his deadly paw.

Stealthily and silently
He stalks his helpless prey
Crouching down amongst the growth
He begins to make his play.

Nick Gardner (11)
Lee Chapel Primary School, Basildon

Being In Exile

I am all alone,
I wish I could go home,
I wish I could go home to the warm, loving smiles of my family.
I wish I could hear the noisy community again
That was once all around me.
I miss my comfortable, cosy bed,
That I once laid in and dreamt happily.
I miss my mother's cuddles and kisses,
All warm and wet.
I hope that one day I will hear an English voice again.
I hope that someone will find me,
I hope that someone will find me and take me home.

Charlotte Toms (10)
Lee Chapel Primary School, Basildon

Special Places

Some places are special to me
Pretty, calm and peaceful
Especially the ones with
Colourful gardens
I love the patterns placed upon the walls
And I think to myself what a
Lovely place to have.

Perfect places just
Lovely for me
Adorable houses
Comforting and special
Everyone wants to be there,
It's somewhere I definitely do.

Ashley Brown (11)
Lee Chapel Primary School, Basildon

Leisure

'What life this, if full of care
we have no time to stand and stare?'

No time to watch your children grow,
Instead you stand in queue shop rows.

No time to take out all the weeds
And then go and plant a few seeds.

No time to listen to tweeting birds,
All you do is speak some words.

'What poor life this, if full of care
we have no time to stand and stare?'

Lauren-Rose Major (9)
Lee Chapel Primary School, Basildon

Being In Exile

Missing the sugarbeat breath of my horse,
Missing the laughter of children.
Wishing that I could have one day with my family,
Wishing I could go round the corner and see the noisy community.
Hoping I could be in my bed warm and cosy,
Hoping I could return home with a warm welcome.
Dreaming that I could taste my mum's roast once more,
Dreaming that my heart didn't feel so sore.

Georgia Savage (11)
Lee Chapel Primary School, Basildon

Snow

Snow slowly falling to the ground
Roads are very icy.
People slip on the path.
The trees are very white.

In the morning when the children rise,
They look out to see the snow.
They feel excited!
They put on their warm clothes.

Benjamin Morris (8)
Lee Chapel Primary School, Basildon

Football

F ootball is what I like to do
O ffside the linesman shouts
O n the ball I run
T he ball rolls over the line, *a goal!*
B ut it's a penalty I got fouled
'A penalty!' cries the referee
'L ovely goal!' screamed the commentator
L eaving the goalkeeper annoyed.

Nathan Blackwell (10)
Lee Chapel Primary School, Basildon

Summer

Boiling sun
Golden beach
Summertime
Summertime
Relaxing holiday
Warm swimming pool
Summertime is here again.

Lily Wu (8)
Marsh Green Primary School, Dagenham

Winter

Quiet hibernation, merry Christmas,
Winter falls, winter falls,
Ruth's birthday, frost bites
Winter falls, winter falls
May the winter praise you,
So let it stay once more
Winter falls!

Ruth Muleya (9)
Marsh Green Primary School, Dagenham

Spring

New leaves
Green shoots
Springtime
Nesting birds
Sudden shower
Springtime is here once more.

Lakhvinder Singh (8)
Marsh Green Primary School, Dagenham

Friends

Friends
Helpful, faithful
Grateful, peaceful, dreadful
My friend is cool
Marvellous.

Luigi Kongo (9)
Marsh Green Primary School, Dagenham

Summer

Freezing drinks
Baking bush fire
Summertime
Summertime
Hot siesta
Summer shouldn't end.

Jack Heywood (9)
Marsh Green Primary School, Dagenham

Hamster

Hamster
Running, climbing,
Jumping, scratching, fighting,
Digging under his sawdust
Sniffing.

Harrison Smith (8)
Marsh Green Primary School, Dagenham

Sweets

Sweets
Scrummy, yummy
Chewy, lovely, tasty
I love my sweets,
Delicious.

Taylor Furneaux (8)
Marsh Green Primary School, Dagenham

Lion

Lion
Growling, sniffing
Prowling, pouncing, running
Eating some delicious meat
Vicious.

Liam Baker (8)
Marsh Green Primary School, Dagenham

My Cat

I have a cat
That plays on her mat
She sometimes wears my hat
One day she came on my lap and sat.

The cat stretched out nice and flat
She purred and purred when I gave her a pat.
With a start up she sat
She leapt across the room to catch a rat.

Katherine M Ellis (8)
Riverside Junior School, Hullbridge

My Dad Has Gone Mad!

Help me!
My dad has gone mad!
He came and worked at my school
He even bought a swimming pool
It was large, colourful, horrible and scary
And some of its sides were actually hairy!

Help me!
My dad has gone mad!
He works in the kitchen with the dinner ladies
He even shared his jelly babies!
He came and shared them around the school
Believe it or not, it was pretty cool!

Help me!
My dad has gone totally mad!
He fell in love . . .
With my head teacher!
Then he gave her a yellow creature!

Help!

Alex Thraves (8)
Riverside Junior School, Hullbridge

The Snowman

The big blob of snow,
The orange carrot nose,
The black beady eyes,
The round black buttons,
The brown chequered hat,
The black buttoned mouth,
The woody brown arms.

What is it?

A Snowman!

Robert Vine (9)
Riverside Junior School, Hullbridge

Snow Is Falling

Snow is falling
Snow is falling
Going everywhere
Children playing
Snowballs flying
Floating through the air.

Building snowmen
Step by step
A great big giant one
I love snow
It makes my feet
And fingers glow.

Sashenka Levey (11)
Riverside Junior School, Hullbridge

My Dog

I have a dog
She sits in the fog
Her big eyes are always there
She always does tricks
And plays with sticks
And sleeps at the top of the stairs.

Sophie Goodliffe (11)
Riverside Junior School, Hullbridge

School

S is for science I like experiments
C is for Christmas plays we have them every year
H is for homework it's sometimes hard
O is for over excited when we have visitors
O is for obstacle courses in PE
L is for listening to class and assembly.

Samantha Tautz (8)
Riverside Junior School, Hullbridge

Friends

Friends will be there
Like a big cuddly bear
Just like people at a funfair,
They do care,
Sometimes they mess up your hair
But never leave, always there.

Friends will be there
You do not have to dare
They're so fair
Letting you be there
When they stroke your brown hair
Friends always share
While you're eating a pear
You will feel like you're in air.

Paige Ruskin (10)
Riverside Junior School, Hullbridge

Bonelli's Eagle

In the mountains soaring high
Bonelli's eagle in the sky
Birds-eye view of all the land
From green grass to seaside sand.

Take a glimpse of feathers speckled
On his lovely, white body mottled
His strong tough wings soft to feel
Grey and black like cold, dull steel.

Shrill piping noise as he calls his mate
To say to her, you missed the bait
The prey is captured on the ground
Look, a meaty rabbit that I found.

Luke Smith (9)
Riverside Junior School, Hullbridge

Once Upon A Time!

Once upon a time,
Humpty Dumpty fell off his wall
Fell on his back
Because of the ball.

Once upon a time
The children play with thrill and happiness,
Then go home
For the rest of the day.

Once upon a time
Jack and Jill went up the high hill
Jack fell down
Then broke his crown.

Once upon a time
The children play with thrill and happiness
Then go home
For the rest of the day.

David Green (10)
Riverside Junior School, Hullbridge

Snow

Snow is precious
Snow is white
Snow is like silk
Silk, a blanket overnight.

It covers the world in a fluffy coat
It glitters and shines
In-between the gracious pines
It is precious, gracious and divine.

It also causes chaos
Kills, destroys
This material evil and sly!

Andrew Gilbey (10)
Riverside Junior School, Hullbridge

Who Will Rule The Universe?

'I'll rule the universe,' said the barking dog,
'Not if I prickle you first,' said the spiky hedgehog.
Then down from the sticky web came the black spider,
And landed on the sleeping tiger.
This frightened the great big cat,
Who got up quickly and stood on the rat.
The rat squeaked and cried out in pain
Then came the thunder and it started to rain.
The wet bat swooped down from the swaying trees
And knocked the hive off the honeybees.
The queen bee was very unhappy and angry
So she sent out her stinging army.
The frog jumped out of the water onto the rock
'Cock-a-doodle-doo,' sang the wise old cock.
It was nearly morning and another new day
What is in store for the animals? No one could say.
Who did rule the universe?

Ryan Hirst (7)
Riverside Junior School, Hullbridge

Henry VIII

Hated, horrible Henry
Giving everyone the chop
Marrying his six wives
Carelessly without thought.

Henry was a lovely boy, once upon a time
Friendly, joyous, a sporty lad
Hunting was his kind

He grew up to become king
Once his brother died
He became a selfish, greedy soul
Eighty thousand dead, for his silly, stupid lies.

Daniel Cole (11)
Riverside Junior School, Hullbridge

Help!

Crunch . . . Crunch . . . Splish . . . Splash . . . Splosh!
I hear them in the distance
They're coming after me!
Help!

Crunch . . . Crunch . . . Splish . . . Splash . . . Splosh!
I see them in the distance
I'm running, I'm running
'Oi you.' They're going to get me
They're coming after me
Help!

Crunch . . . Crunch . . . Splish . . . Splash . . . Splosh!
They're right behind me
They grab my shoulder . . .
'You dropped your wallet,' they pant.

James Wood (10)
Riverside Junior School, Hullbridge

Sweets

I love sweets that are in my tummy
Eat them quick before my mummy.

I love sweets because they're nice
Including the chocolate mice.

I love sweets wrapped in paper
Because you can save them for later.

I love sweets with toffee inside
When I eat these I always hide.

I love sweets, lots of sweets
They're a great Friday treat.

I love sweets!

Adam Rice (7)
Riverside Junior School, Hullbridge

The Aliens

An alien came to town
And landed on the ground.
Everybody began to run around
They were crying and screaming to get away.
'Go away! Go back home!' they began to say.
He was unhappy to hear what they just said,
'My name is Ed,' the alien said.
'Have you met my brother Zed?'
'We're sorry that we were mean to you,' they cried
The aliens began to smile then they waved
Bye-bye!

Joe Hall (8)
Riverside Junior School, Hullbridge

My Special Key

I put my magical key inside the keyhole in my front door
I see a bright new house shining in front of me.
Next I walk outside into the garden
I see beautiful colours all around me.
When I go to bed I have one last look at the key
And I can see it glowing in the dark as brightly as can be.

Louise Turner (9)
Riverside Junior School, Hullbridge

My Hamster

My hamster has small feet
My hamster loves to eat.
I fill up his bowl every day
And he likes to come and play.
My hamster is fluffy
And his friend is Muffy.

Amanda Ambrose (9)
Riverside Junior School, Hullbridge

I Want To Be. . .

I want to be a pop star
With a gleaming red sports car
Going on lots of well-known shows
Wearing a wardrobe of incredible clothes.

I want to be a baker
A cake, cookie and sweet maker.
Every lively day,
I will eat lots of sweets without having to pay!

I want to be a dancer
I'll climb the rainbow and dance like the amazing reindeer Prancer.
I'll tap and clap all day long
Maybe I might sing a catchy song.

I want to be . . .

Alice Baker (9)
Riverside Junior School, Hullbridge

Libraries

Libraries are fun
There are lots that can be done
Also lots of different kinds of books
From Jack and Hill
To the baby seal
Libraries are a quiet place
Where the books look you right in the face.

The people in the library care
Lots of people share
When I'm there I eat a pear
Whenever I read a book I feel like I'm in the air
There are books everywhere
Some books are rare.

Chantelle Ann Hand (10)
Riverside Junior School, Hullbridge

Roller Coaster

I'm standing here,
Waiting in line
'Come on!' I call,
I'm running out of time.

Slowly and steadily
The line goes down
This line is so long
I can see my own town.

At last I'm here
I'm on the carriage
I see a bride
Heading for her marriage.

The ride has started
I'm upside down
My hands go up
I'm screaming aloud.

I'm off the ride
Dizzy as can be
I see another roller coaster
Here we go, *weee!*

Amy Jones (11)
Riverside Junior School, Hullbridge

Football

I can kick a ball high
I can kick a ball low
I can kick the ball where I want it to go.

In the goal!

I can kick the ball up and down
I can kick the ball along the ground.

I can kick the ball when it's wet
I can kick the ball into the net.

Connor Clift (7)
Riverside Junior School, Hullbridge

The Stormy Night

All the animals scamper
as the night gets damper,
they sit and they wonder
if tonight there could be thunder.

Rain starts to fall hard on the ground
the fox searches for food not making a sound,
a flash of lightning lights up the sky
the birds start to shiver way up high.

The thunder starts to crash and boom
the badgers hope it will stop soon
the baby squirrels run for cover
they know they're safe with their mother.

By the minute the storm gets quieter
as the evening sky gets lighter,
the sun rises as the storm starts to rest
the birds are stirring in their nest.

The rabbits were frightened for so long
they were happy that the storm had gone
the foxes laid out in the sun
all the animals had so much fun.

Lauren Bibby (9)
Riverside Junior School, Hullbridge

The Moon Is So Bright

The moon is so bright, it's like a flashing light.
It's as big as a baboon but will turn half soon.
I like to look at it when I'm in bed
It shines on top of the garden shed.
If you want the moon just come to me
You can see how lovely it can be.
So you don't have to go to bed dark . . .
You can have the moon while the dogs bark.

Melissa Keene (7)
Riverside Junior School, Hullbridge

Storm

The clouds are murky pieces of gloom,
The lightning is a flickering firework,
The thunder is a reckless roar,
The night is a violent explosion,
The midnight is a boom of darkness.

The storm is a terrifying monster,
The river is a swirling tornado,
The wind is a petrifying crash,
The rain is a rushing dam,
The hurricane is a sheet of black.

April Byott (9)
Riverside Junior School, Hullbridge

Santa Is Here

Santa is here
Santa is here
Rummaging through his black sack
Choosing our presents.

His sleigh is led by Rudolph
With his red shining nose
Blazing in the moon's light.

Lucy Williamson (9)
Riverside Junior School, Hullbridge

School, School, School

School, school, school
I am fond of school
My school is kind
It is fond of me
I try not to get in trouble
School, school, school.

Dermot Dobson (10)
Riverside Junior School, Hullbridge

Dark Night

Wolves howl, shadows prance,
Over the fence I peek.
Skeletons rise in a clear fine mist,
Creaky gates open.
I look through the corridors
And up the stairs,
Shadows dance
But nobody is there.
But down in the cellars
Monsters groan,
I begin to wonder,
Am I alone?

Jessica Monk (8)
Riverside Junior School, Hullbridge

My Daddy

My dad is mad
He's not good at fishing
That makes him sad.

He wants to catch a big fish
The size of a dish
That would be his wish.

Elysia Anthony (8)
Riverside Junior School, Hullbridge

Wind

Wind wind everywhere
In the air and in the sky
Never in space
Daring to blow down trees
Sometimes blowing through your house.

Lewis Groombridge (8)
Riverside Junior School, Hullbridge

Snow

Snow is white
It glitters in the light
It tumbles down from the sky
All the birds screech, 'Bye-bye'
It falls
It falls
It falls.

Snow is fun
It melts in the sun
But when it turns to ice
It's not very nice
It falls
It falls
It falls.

When we have a snowstorm
It lay across the lawn
It covers the farmer's corn
At the crack of dawn
It falls
It falls
It falls.

Snow is falling from the sky
When it melts it's not very dry
In the sun it glistens
To the birds' song we listen
It falls
It falls
It falls.

Snow! Snow! Snow!

Taylor Gouldsmith (9)
Riverside Junior School, Hullbridge

Horses

Gorgeous horse
Galloping by
Mane flowing
Tail swishing
Thundering feet
Beautiful colour
Happy as can be
Hear him say
Food! Food!
I want food
With his eyes shining
From reflecting the sunlight.

Look at that horse
Doing its best trick of course
But a bit silly of course.

Beth Goessen (8)
Riverside Junior School, Hullbridge

Goldfish Fred

He is 110 years old in fish years
He is 7 years old in human years.
He darts through the water
Like a person in a swimming race.
He loves his food
He does not speak at all
His name is Fred.
He's got shiny scales.
He wiggles through the water
Like a slithery snake.
He tricks me when I watch him.
I really like my fish Fred.

Dean Bonning (8)
Riverside Junior School, Hullbridge

The Wonders Of The World

The gushing of the water
The singing of the birds
The leaves as they fall
The wonders of the world.

The waterfall
The caves so dark
Out in the sunlight
Or in the night sky.

The birds as they sing
The snakes as they slither
The ponies as they gallop
The wonders of the world.

Fire, water
Sun, moon
Hot, cold
The wonders of the world.

Jodie Whittington (9)
Riverside Junior School, Hullbridge

Oscar

Oscar is a rabbit he is fluffy
Oscar is cuddly he is puffy
Oscar is the best he is nice
Oscar I love him there is nothing on him
Not even lice.
In April he will be one years of age
My grandad built him a play cage
He lives in the garden in my shed
He is always warm in his cuddly bed.

I love Oscar.

Katy Brown (8)
Riverside Junior School, Hullbridge

The Haunted House

There once was a mansion
It was haunted by ghosts
No one ever went there
Not even near the posts.

If you do go in you won't come out
Not even the ghost's niece
She wouldn't dare go there
Even with the police.

Someone called Jack
Was dared to go in
So in he stepped
And stood on a pin.

Although he didn't care
Not at all
Because he was playing with his favourite toy
A bouncy ball.

Robin Mead (9)
Riverside Junior School, Hullbridge

My Home

Walking home in the night,
Walking home in the night,
Looking into homes
Seeing all the lights
Lights in the windows
Lights in the doors
Lights up the stairs
Lights on all the floors
But my home is odd
My home is strange
The moment I reach home I see that it has changed.

Jordan Swinge (7)
Riverside Junior School, Hullbridge

Santa

Santa you're good, Santa you're nice
You bring presents no matter the price.

You slip our presents under the tree
And you eat the mince pies which were left by me.

Santa tells Rudolph to be as quiet as a mouse
As he sits there patiently on top of our house.

Thank you dear Santa for being so kind
Just one more thing, bear my hamster in mind!

Megan Smith (8)
Riverside Junior School, Hullbridge

Fish

Fish glides spiral twirls twisting round and round
Gleaming eyes glow in the dark of swishing water
Beautiful sparkling rainbow scales shimmering in the
Shining blue sea
Fish' fins whoosh from side to side
Tiny eyes gleam and stare at you.
Fish blow transparent bubbles through the invisible air.
When the sun sets the moon shines
Fish have a sparkle in their eyes.

Holly Williams (8)
Riverside Junior School, Hullbridge

The Beauty Of The World

As the great crocodiles snap in the morning
The kingfisher chirps along a happy tune
As the seals slither and slide in agony to get to the sea
The sharks, fish and dolphins swim along happily.

Connor Baker (10)
Riverside Junior School, Hullbridge

The Vikings

The Vikings were horrible, they came in their long boats to invade.
They murdered the Anglo Saxons and came here to explore.
They stole the monks' gold from Lindisfarne Monastery.
They settled in fast and thought they had won
Until King Alfred's army surrounded the Vikings' camp.
King Gathrum turned Christian when he saw their Anglo Saxon
army and surrendered.
King Canute returned to England with the Swedish Danes,
By that time King Alfred was ready for the Danes.
They battled and King Alfred won
He won the title 'Great'
Bringing peace and justice to England.

Harry Cole (8)
Riverside Junior School, Hullbridge

My Game Boy

I like to play my Game Boy
Every chance I get
All my friends and family say it's my pet
I say don't be silly it just isn't so
I think of it as my best mate, but don't let the
Others know!
My favourite game is Sonic.

Jason Jones (8)
Riverside Junior School, Hullbridge

My Grandad

My grandad is always playing darts
He thinks he is a winner
But my nanna says he's not very good
He would be better if he was thinner.

Chelsie Benson (7)
Riverside Junior School, Hullbridge

Pets

Pets are cute
Pets are cool
Don't you think they are?
Pets are silly
Pets are pretty
The very best by far!
Pets can dance
Pets can run
All around the house
Pets can jump
Pets can fly
Big to small as a mouse.

Nicole Clayden (10)
Riverside Junior School, Hullbridge

The Castle

A man lived in a
dark
dirty
spooky
cold
little bit broken
wet castle
but he liked it there!

Ryan Beckwith (7)
Riverside Junior School, Hullbridge

My Garden

I spend hours picking flowers
There are humming bees and enormous trees
At night I see bats, catching moths and gnats
My garden is brilliant.

Bonnie Degenhard (7)
Riverside Junior School, Hullbridge

The Wonders Of The World!

Beauty and wonders are amongst us,
In very unique shapes and sizes,
A waterfall brushes against rocks,
Then crashes down to meet more,
Sunsets by lakes and rivers reflect to make a rainbow.

Dolphins are mystical creatures
Only to be seen in moonlight,
They used to live on land once
But now they roam the sea,
Stars shining brightly at night
Next to the moon's light.

Hedgehogs scurry quickly for winter,
Crispy snow when the cold comes,
Making snowmen in luscious snow
Fluffy lambs in the spring bouncing around like
                                  little bunnies.

Emily Pearson (11)
Riverside Junior School, Hullbridge

The Typhoon

The storm is approaching
I can feel it
The typhoon has struck
It's a raging intruder
Thunder is a crashing drum
There is a cyclone spinning around the town.

Every now and then I hear a rumble of thunder
This typhoon is working its way around
The weather is spine-chilling
Cars are crashing
Homes are falling
It's not over yet . . .

George Flanagan (11)
Riverside Junior School, Hullbridge

My Amazing Garden

The grass is so green
It has to be seen
The trees are so tall
And the flowers are small
The pond is deep
That's where the fish sleep
When the rabbit goes in the run
He has some fun
The birds sing a song
But they don't stay for long
Because the big black cat
Watches them from his mat
We have a big shed
And it's painted red
The worms go underground
And they wriggle around
But the best bit of all
It's where I play when I get home from school.

Hayley Deeks (8)
Riverside Junior School, Hullbridge

Animals

Rubbery dolphins swim and swirl,
Grey squirrels when hibernating curl,
Slow spiky hedgehogs looking for insects and snails
The grey-brown koala eating damp leaves off a gum tree,
And a seal hunting for fish in the deep blue sea.

The tall elegant giraffe has round beady eyes as dark as
The night,
And lions will fight for a meal,
Tigers will pounce rapidly onto their kill,
Terrified by this antelopes would scatter,
And hyenas would chatter.

Kim Radmore (11)
Riverside Junior School, Hullbridge

Fairyality

In the spring, wonderful flowers
open up to show a dainty baby flower
fairy awake.
In the summer, these tiny tots
flutter in the golden rays of sunshine.
In the autumn, the sweet fairy girls and boys
dance in the red and golden leaves.
In the winter, they bounce across the clean,
white and cold blanket that they have
never seen before.

Ella George (10)
Riverside Junior School, Hullbridge

My Old Teddy Bear

I found my old teddy bear up in the loft
I snuggled in bed with him because he was so soft.
I looked in the morning, he wasn't there
Mr Teddy Bear wasn't anywhere.
Perhaps he didn't want my cuddles anymore
I climbed out of bed, there he was,
. . . On the floor.

Georgia Davies (8)
Riverside Junior School, Hullbridge

Wind

Wind fills the sky with horrid howls
Wind is freezing and horrible and cold
Wind blows from tree to tree
Making everybody very cold
All I hear outside is the wind whistling
Giving me a fright, in the night.

Nathan Adewunmi (8)
Riverside Junior School, Hullbridge

Race In Space

I went to space
in a race
with a vroommm!
and a boommm!
with two friends called Splish and Sposh.

First we went through Mars Bar
and then the Milky Way
by the time we got to Galaxy
we'd been flying for a day.

We slept among the shooting stars in a
chocolate bed, with a marshmallow pillow
under our heads
we snoozed and snored the night away.

The moon cockerel crowed night to day
with my alien friends here in space
I think I might . . .
stay!

Sonny Horwell (8)
Riverside Junior School, Hullbridge

Playtime Fun

Noisy
Crowded
Skipping
Running
Laughter
Whispers
Girls
Screaming
Shouting
And that's what you call playtime *fun!*

Keye Frith (7)
Riverside Junior School, Hullbridge

Lightning

Lightning flies through the air
Lightning crashes into the air
Lightning flashes in the night, and gives me a fright.
So I switch on my light
Dogs howl through the night
Cats miaow and foxes scamper into the light.
The city turns bright,
As the people switch on their lights.
Everything goes quiet
So I switch off my light.

Keeleigh Goldring (7)
Riverside Junior School, Hullbridge

Teachers

Teachers, teachers everywhere
Teachers, teachers in the air
Teachers, teachers sit on chairs
Teachers, teachers have big hair
Teachers, teachers in the sky
Teachers, teachers fly so high.

Lauren Putinas (8)
Riverside Junior School, Hullbridge

My Dog

I have a dog called Ozzy
Who runs round and round he jumps
Up at the gate and makes an awful sound.
He likes to go for walks and stop to have a talk.
Ozzy's not very tall cause he's very small and his
Favourite toy is a ball.

Zoe Streeter (8)
Riverside Junior School, Hullbridge

My Annoying Brother

My annoying brother thinks he's cool
But really he is the dumbest of them all.
His main thing is his hair
Just looking at it gives me quite a scare.
He puts on his hat and it flattens his hair
People give him quite a stare.
My brother is really lazy
But he is quite so crazy.
My brother goes to sleep and
He dumps his clothes onto a heap.
My brother goes to school
And swims in a swimming pool.
My annoying brother thinks he's fun
But he's really dumb.
He has no friend
Because he drives everyone round the bend.
He climbs a tree and
Gets stung by a bee.
He doesn't like cats
But he will pick up lots of rats.
He does not think about his hair,
And shoves gel on without any care.

Emily Williams (8)
Riverside Junior School, Hullbridge

Stormy Weather

The clouds are grey and bold
The thunder is a lion roaring
The lightning is as bright as a firework
The night is a petrifying horror
The hurricane is a reckless gale
The storm is a crashing drum
The river is a flooding sudden
The rain is a strong tornado.

Alicia Morrow (10)
Riverside Junior School, Hullbridge

Tiger!

There's a tiger in the jungle
I'll tell you what it's like
Its teeth are sharp spikes
Its claws are pointed shiny blades
Its eyes are more colourful than a rainbow.

Ryan Williams (11)
Riverside Junior School, Hullbridge

Dogs

Dogs, dogs are my favourite pet
Dogs, dogs sometimes are ill then go to the vet
There are some that are fat and some that are thin
They're the ones that eat all the greens.

Don't you love dogs?

Fay Oxby (8)
Riverside Junior School, Hullbridge

Space

S pace, space it's so nice
P laces are so bright at night
A tmosphere is all around
C ircles are the planets I found
E verywhere you look is space!

Marcus Neophytou (8)
Riverside Junior School, Hullbridge

The Snow

The snow comes drifting down from the moonlit sky,
It lands on the ground in a soft crunchy layer.
It sits there still and silent just glistening in the moonlight.

Chloe Humphreys (10)
Riverside Junior School, Hullbridge

My Cat Fluffy

My cat is fluffy
My cat is so cute
She plays with me all the time
Scratches me, pulls my hair,
She is brown and black.
Her name is Fluffy
She is only a little kitten
She is so cute.

Leah Caiger (9)
Riverside Junior School, Hullbridge

Cats

Some cats are big and some are small
Some cats are short and some are tall
Some cats are fluffy and some are smooth
When it's dark some cats look like green eyed shadows
And most cats want to sleep all day.
I like cats do you?

Do you like cats?

Lauren Watts (7)
Riverside Junior School, Hullbridge

Alien

There's an alien in my bedroom, Mum
I'll tell you what it's like,
Its head is like a giant squidgy ball
Its eyes are big and red
Its legs are like jelly cubes
Its teeth are as blunt as scissors
Its body is like a blown up water balloon
And that is what it looked like!

Jo Serretiello (10)
Riverside Junior School, Hullbridge

Henry VIII

Henry VIII had six wives
Married Catherine of Aragon,
'Divorce, divorce,' says Henry,
'You're too old for me.'

'Anne Boleyn I do,' says Henry,
'Although that extra finger
You've been going off with other men,
You've betrayed me.'
Henry sniggered, scowled and said,
'You're being arrested and beheaded tonight.'

'I'm marrying you Jane Seymour,
Although you were Anne's maid,
A Son I have!
A Son I have at last!
Name him Edward,
Name him Prince Edward.
Jane Seymour who gave birth to my Son
Has died, has died.'

'Anne of Cleaves,
I love you, I love you,
Anne of Cleaves,
I hate you, I hate you, I'm divorcing you.'

'Katherine Howard you're marrying me,
I don't care what you say,
Katherine Howard you're being executed,
I don't care what you say.'

'Katherine Parr you're marrying me,
When my brother dies,
Katherine Parr I love you loads,
Although I'm about to die.'

Anna Dixon (10)
Riverside Junior School, Hullbridge

Special Days

Did you know that through the years
we shed some happy and sad tears
Oh what joy Christmas, Easter and birthdays bring
there's presents, chocolates, cards what wonderful things.
We share our love on Valentine's Day
where words are written things we need to say.
These are the days we need to remember
remember, remember the 5th of November.
We get fireworks in different colours so bright
which makes Guy Fawkes such a special delight.
To end this poem one thing I must say
enjoy yourself, be happy whatever the day.

Samantha Delves (8)
Riverside Junior School, Hullbridge

Deep Deep In The Garden

Flowers, flowers, you have a lot of power
Trees, trees you're stronger than the breeze
Pond, pond you're as long as a swan
Fish, fish you look nice on my dish, especially
When I wish
Wish, wish, wish . . .

Georgina Goddard (7)
Riverside Junior School, Hullbridge

Cinders

I have a horse called Cinders who's getting on in years
When I leave her at the end of the day you can almost see my tears.
When I rode her the other day I was very happy
But did Cinders really care?
When I finally leave her, it is always very late
I'm sad because she is my best mate.

Danielle Jones (8)
Riverside Junior School, Hullbridge

Fish

Fish can be different shapes
and different colours.
Fish sometimes have green
gleaming eyes in the reflecting
wavy water.
Fish sometimes have shiny
beautiful ails.
Fish swim peacefully in the
clean bright tank filled with fun,
food and friends.

Jessica Goody (9)
Riverside Junior School, Hullbridge

Pets!

P ets are cute and cuddly things
E very day they snuggle up against me
T imes when pets are sad and lonely
S pend some time with your pets.

If you have a pet
make sure you love
it to bits.

Katie Watkins (10)
Riverside Junior School, Hullbridge

Fireworks

Bang, crackle, zoom and whoosh,
It's firework night again.
Children screaming, adults shouting,
'Ooh!'
Fireworks booming across the sky
Sizzle, crackle, zoom.

Suzanna Todd (8)
Riverside Junior School, Hullbridge

Fat Cats

Fat cats, fat cats everywhere,
Big and round and covered in hair.
Dawdle, dawdle, sleep, sleep, sleep,
What a lazy, tiresome life he keeps.
Drinks milk and eats mice,
And tries to chase the woodlice.
Can't even run, can't even pounce,
Can't even skip, can't even bounce.
So now you know what fat cats are like,
So never ask them to take a hike!

Gemma Lloyd (9)
Riverside Junior School, Hullbridge

Food

When I went to the supermarket the other day
My tummy rumbled all the way.
I could not stop it, it just went on and on
By the time I got there the food on the shelves was gone.

After that I went home
I was starving for a Toblerone.
I ate everything in the cupboards
And everything in the freezer.
Also after that I had a malteser.

Amy Pighini (9)
Riverside Junior School, Hullbridge

Dance

My name is Jess, I love to dance,
To twirl around the stage and prance,
My favourite things are jazz and tap,
But I also like to sing and rap.

Jessica Tyrrell (10)
Riverside Junior School, Hullbridge

Clidy

She was born with *Clidy* beside her
The dog was called *Clidy*
Clidy was fluffy, smooth and straight
He could run the marathon
She could walk with *Clidy*
She could play with *Clidy*
But when he was sleeping don't wake him up
Clidy loved her
He really did
She loved *Clidy*
She really did.

Gemma Jones (8)
Riverside Junior School, Hullbridge

Snow

Snow drifting down gently in the middle of the night,
Covering the world in a twinkling white
The snow keeps on falling
Every flake a different shape
Waiting until the morning when the children wake,
In the morning, the children shout with glee,
'The snow has come, yippee!'

Laura Barrett (11)
Riverside Junior School, Hullbridge

Love

If love was a colour it would be red
If love was an animal it would be a soft kitten
If love was a type of weather it would be the sun
If love was a shape it would be a heart
If love was a musical instrument it would be a harp.

Ben Cox (9)
Riverside Junior School, Hullbridge

Holiday

Down at the beach
We swim in the sea
Building sandcastles
My sister and me
We lay on our towels
Soaking up the sun
Eating ice cream
And having lots of fun
We go snorkelling, surfing
Riding the waves,
Then me and Dad
Go exploring the caves,
And then Mum says
With a sigh and a frown,
'It's time to go home,'
As the sun goes down.

Rachel Hilliard (7)
Riverside Junior School, Hullbridge

The Witches Of Hallowe'en

The witches of Hallowe'en
ooh woo
Their faces are black and green
ooh woo

In the middle of the night
They give you such a fright

> *ooh woo*

The witches of Hallowe'en
They give you such a scare
They *blow off all your hair*
The witches of Hallowe'en
ooh woo.

Chloe Shayes (9)
Riverside Junior School, Hullbridge

The Four Seasons

The wind is dead, the sun is warm,
Plants are growing, lambs are born
Birds are flying, trees are bright,
Deer are running, what a sight.

The wind has gone, the sun is hot
Everyone is burning, so animals trot
The sun is up, in the sky
The things on the ground, are very dry.

The leaves are falling, to the ground
The animals are making not a single sound.
The birds are digging for their food
The green grass is totally dewed.

The snow is falling, the ice is frozen
Everyone is cold, doors are closed
The crystals hang, the birds are not singing
The sun has gone, the bells are ringing.

Dale Bliss (10)
Riverside Junior School, Hullbridge

Animals

Wild cats creep around,
Black baboons bounce on the ground,
Crafty crocodiles open their jaws,
And lazy lions lay down the laws.

Grumpy gorillas fight over their meals,
Careful camels walk up the sandy hills,
Enormous elephants gracefully walk,
And laughing hyenas sound like they talk.

Dancing dolphins swim and swirl,
Smooth seals have eyes like pearls,
Giant giraffes munch high in the trees,
And elegant emus have long legs with knobbly knees.

Kerry Radmore (11)
Riverside Junior School, Hullbridge

Invaders From Outer Space

Invaders from outer space
When will they come?
You would have to admit
It would be quite fun
What if they were already here?
What about your mum?

If you were abducted
What would they do?
If they came to Earth
Would they come for you?
The teachers seem quite weird
If they could turn into goo
Would they be friendly?

If you were people
Would they like how we look?
Would they be the same
Or would they be smart
Or do they even exist?

Sam Bottrill (10)
Riverside Junior School, Hullbridge

My Sister

My sister is annoying
She drives me up the wall
She's always angry
And never cares.
That's my sister!
My sister is fourteen
She's bigger than I am
I still argue with her
And I still get cross with her
But there's nothing I can do about it.

Georgia Hellen (9)
Riverside Junior School, Hullbridge

The Three-Eyed Monster

He's got a big tall horn
On top of his head,
He gets very grumpy
When he gets out of bed.
He lives on Planet Barno
With his friends and family,
He's going on holiday soon
To Planet Camerly.
Sometimes he's happy
Sometimes he's cruel
He fills his rocket
With jelly jet fuel.
He's got two noses
And three eyes,
He smells very badly
Because of the flies.
He is smelly
Like strawberry jelly.

Lauren Foley (8)
Riverside Junior School, Hullbridge

Sweets

Liquorice is red
It tastes nice when you're fed
Not when you've just got out of bed
It tastes better at night
But sometimes it gives you a fright
Yummy yummy
Says my tummy
I eat it, down it goes
I eat so much my belly overflows
It tastes so nice
So do chocolate mice!

Rebeca Goody (11)
Riverside Junior School, Hullbridge

Animals Around The School

On my way to school today
I saw something in a rapid way
Was it a cheetah or a rabbit I saw?
Going through my classroom door
Was it pink or was it black?
All I saw was its back
But I decided to follow the animal through a little crack
But when I lost the animal I fell down a crack
But when I got out of school I didn't know what place I was at.

Chloe Pierce (9)
Riverside Junior School, Hullbridge

Different Types Of Animals

A nimals run wild and free
N ature blossoms everywhere,
I nsects bounce around happily
M ammals munch on juicy grass
A lbatross fly from place to place,
L eopards leap from tree to tree
S nakes slither in and out of the grass.

Lysette Stepaniuk (10)
Riverside Junior School, Hullbridge

Casinos

Down the crowded casinos
There's tarty tattoos
With booming banjos
Banging bongos and pretty pianos
Singing solos
Fantastic fiestas
Soft sofas
But be careful, there's catching cameras.

Ellie Gatehouse (10)
Riverside Junior School, Hullbridge

Racehorses

I stand proud and ready within the barrier.

I'm hot and uncomfortable in my clothing but I don't
Show it as other horses and riders would stare and mumble.

Meanwhile a smartly dressed man lifts a small grey object.

It fires sharply and frightens us.

The barriers release suddenly.

We canter insanely, my moron tail swishing in the wind.

While I'm still galloping, I twist my head to itch my clammy neck,
I see a golden hot-tempered horse rushing past,
Painfully her saddle catches me.

My rider sees I'm wounded yet he urges me on
So I race as hard as I can down the turf leaving others behind.

Sophie Prosser (11)
Riverside Junior School, Hullbridge

Seasons

Flowers dancing in the spring breeze
Leaves swaying in the autumn wind
Snow falling covering the grass
Flowers making the grass look dull
Leaves making red, orange, brown carpets,
Newborn wildlife making its appearance into the world,
Butterflies swoop in and out of flowers,
The red sunset making the streams glitter,
The wind curves up waves as big as twenty-one storey building,
Water gushing down waterfalls,
Flowers died in the autumn chill,
Rain pouring down on the wildlife,
Floods killing wildlife,
The blue flowers are the blue sky.

Thomas Vine (11)
Riverside Junior School, Hullbridge

Attention!

I get ready in my army clothes,
Off to training we will go.
We're the soldiers we line up straight,
We stand at ease so we will wait.
Along comes the general training starts,
Off to the assault course we will march.
Through the nets and up the ropes,
Wriggling quickly to the slopes.
Down the slopes and in the lake,
Freezing cold we shiver and shake.
Now to our feet we finally get,
Lining up all soaking wet.
Back to base we finally go,
Marching slowly to and fro.
Back at base the general says,
'Get your supper, then go to bed!'
So I got my supper and off to bed
I say goodnight and that's the end.

Goodnight!

George Williams (10)
Riverside Junior School, Hullbridge

My Dad

My dad snores
It echoes round the room
My mum said, 'Hark at that racket!'
He snores in bed
He snores on the sofa
Watching EastEnders
He rumbles during
I'm A Celebrity Get Me Out Of Here.
He works really late
Sometimes he's gone all night
He's a lorry driver
That's why he snores at home.

Matthew Croucher (11)
Riverside Junior School, Hullbridge

Party

Dancing divas
With terrific tattoos
People having fun with nothing to lose
Pizzas as big as a frying pan
People dancing need a fan
Little sisters waiting for the party races
People chewing on sour laces
Bring this altogether you get
A great big . . .
                    Party!

Sian Batcheler (11)
Riverside Junior School, Hullbridge

It Is A Snowy Day

It is a snowy day
I see children playing I too play
A squidgy, sloppy snowball hit me
The person that threw it was called Lee.
The next day I woke up ready for another fun day
I looked out the window and it was gone
It had melted!
Oh no!

Eireann Beardon (9)
Riverside Junior School, Hullbridge

The Candle

In the dark room
A flickering light
Illuminates the room,
And it is dripping wax on the table
Gradually the light gets smaller and smaller,
Until it goes out and the room is left in darkness . . .

Chelsea Furr (9)
Riverside Junior School, Hullbridge

Animals

Tiger, tiger, where are you?
I am at the London Zoo.
Help me! Help me!
Run away
There is a monster in my way.
Help me, help me, he is hairy
He is ugly
He is scary.

Ellis Berry (7)
St Margaret's CE Primary School, Basildon

Football

We kick and shoot
Wearing our studded boots
We dribble the ball
And wait for a call.
Tackle the player who tries to score
As we do not want a draw.
As all the fans cheer and roar
When our team scores.

Jonathan Coles (7)
St Margaret's CE Primary School, Basildon

My Horse Velvet

V is for Velvet a cuddly pony
E is for Ellie her foal
L is for love all the family wants
V is for Velvet who likes walks in forests
E is for Ellie trotting around the field
T is for Tally Velvet's mum.

Molly Aparicio (7)
St Margaret's CE Primary School, Basildon

On The Beach

Children running on the beach
Spades and buckets in their hands
Playing in the sand.

Water splashing on the shore
Seagulls flying in the sky
Food awaiting nearby.

Ice cream, lollies up for sale
Mum and Dad queue up to pay
Back to the car we're on our way
Home we go had a great day.

James Holdsworth (7)
St Margaret's CE Primary School, Basildon

Homework

H omework is for home
O h, oh
M aths good at
E nglish bad at
W riting, writing not again
O h, oh
R eading, reading
K now it, know it.

Reeve Peters (8)
St Margaret's CE Primary School, Basildon

Star light

Star light star bright
Angel light angel bright
So good so nice
So pretty.

Declan Corder (7)
St Margaret's CE Primary School, Basildon

Seasons

Summer is hot
Winter is cold
Autumn leaves fall off trees
Springtime flowers grow and grow
My favourite season is when it snows.

Joshua Coles (7)
St Margaret's CE Primary School, Basildon

A Teacher From Leeds

There once was a teacher from Leeds
Who swallowed a packet of seeds
The children all laughed
Because he looked daft
Oh that silly old teacher from Leeds.

Chloe Hannaford (8)
St Margaret's CE Primary School, Basildon

Once There Was A Man Called Pain

Once there was a man called Pain
He liked to visit Spain
He got a bump on his head
He thought he was dead
That was the last of Pain.

Henry Keune (8)
St Margaret's CE Primary School, Basildon

In Or Out Shake It About

In or out shake it about
Do you want to dance?
Do you want to go to France?
If you do go to the loo.

Courtney Brunning (8)
St Margaret's CE Primary School, Basildon

Dragons

She lives in a dark cave
She has four tiny babies
Her name is Teara
If you meet her you will see
Spiky, black, hairy, red and green
Patchy skin
She has long sharp claws
Big floppy wings, pointy teeth
She creeps on webbed feet
Teara hunts in the spooky
For food for her babies.
She breathes smoke from her nostrils
All other creatures get scared.

Lauren Pink (8)
St Margaret's CE Primary School, Basildon

A Lovely Poem

I have a friend called Lilly
Who likes a boy called Billy.
They are quite funny,
They each have a pet bunny.
Lilly and Billy carried their bunnies to school,
Their friends thought it was very cool.

Kristy Amis (8)
St Margaret's CE Primary School, Basildon

The Man With The Broken Clock

There once was a man named Rick
Whose clock had lost its tick
So he bought a new clock
That had its tick-tock
And then that was the end of his old tock-tick.

Callum Launder (8)
St Margaret's CE Primary School, Basildon

The Cat With The Red Hat

A cat was sitting on a mat
Wearing a hat but one day
He got off the
Mat and took
Off the hat
The next day he went out
To play and he saw his
Friend Jack who
Had a black
Sack on his back.

Leah Oakes (8)
St Margaret's CE Primary School, Basildon

The Monkey Called Chum

There once was a monkey called Chum
Who loved to drink pints of rum
He loved eating chips while swinging his hips
And loved to wiggle his bum.
He said to his mum who was called Mrs Fun
'I love to wiggle by bum.'

Connor Sturt (8)
St Margaret's CE Primary School, Basildon

About My Family

My mum and dad were in the house
Then my mum screamed 'cause she saw a mouse,
My dad was in his room shouting, 'Boom, boom!'
My brother was mad with a book in his hand
I was reading a book about a cook,
My other brother was singing with Oz.

Ben Callaghan (8)
St Margaret's CE Primary School, Basildon

Chocolate Dream

Once I saw a Curly Wurly
Acting like a twirly girly,
Hey stay back I have a Toblerone
And if you don't mind I'd like to eat it alone.
Now would you like a Kit-Kat?
Yes I'd like to feed it to my rat.
Look at my precious Smarties,
They just love parties,
And look at my sweet Rolos,
Eating mini polos.

Keelan Roebuck (9)
St Margaret's CE Primary School, Basildon

Chocolate Bars

Bounty I come from a different county
Mars you can get there by flying cars
After Eight don't be late
Kit-Kat the cat got the rat
Aero turn down the stereo
Flake great with cake
Dream of a loud scream
Curly Wurly it's very twirly.

Sophie Parkinson (9)
St Margaret's CE Primary School, Basildon

Mr Flocket

There was a man called Mr Flocket
Who went up in an enormous rocket
His tongue went *clang!*
He went *bang!*
And he ended up in his mum's pocket.

Reece Brown (8)
St Margaret's CE Primary School, Basildon

World War III

In World War III a disastrous place
The soldiers are planning in a base.

Blood squirting everywhere
Going up into the air.

Captain says, 'Fire at will'
But he doesn't know his soldiers are ill.

Bang, bang, the guns went
And the bombs making a dent.

'I surrender,' the soldier said
Behind them, soldiers are dead.

Kyle Boshell (9)
St Margaret's CE Primary School, Basildon

Animals

A for alligator
N for natterjack
I for iguana
M for monkey
A for ant
L for leopard
S for snake.

Nadine Gray (8)
St Margaret's CE Primary School, Basildon

Prance And France

There was a man called Prance
Who likes to go to France,
He split his pants
Got bit by ants
And that was his last chance.

Benjamin Taylor (8)
St Margaret's CE Primary School, Basildon

A Chocolate Poem

I ate some cake, on it was Flake,
When M&Ms
Came out of my pens.
My Twisters
Gave me no blisters,
When Bounty,
Was available in every county.
Smarties said, 'Let's throw some parties.'
While Twix
Is up to no tricks.
Kit-Kat
Beat that!

Leah Wright (9)
St Margaret's CE Primary School, Basildon

Life

1, 2, 3, I'm doing PE
4, 5, 6, I'm doing the splits
7, 8, 9, doing the nine times tables
10, 11, 12, you can do it as well
13, 14, 15. where have you been?
16, 17, 18, I like my team
19, 20, 21, now this poem is all done.

Luke Staszewski (8)
St Margaret's CE Primary School, Basildon

The Cat

A cat that sat on a wall fell off
And ended up in a hall.
He set up a wail,
Which made me go pale
I'd rather have a dog after all.

Matthew Young (8)
St Margaret's CE Primary School, Basildon

My Melty Chocolate

Toffee Crisp makes me lisp
Pharaoh aero makes me scaro
Munchie Crunchie makes me hungry
Revels are devils
Yorkie is so dorkie
Maltesers are for geezers
Ripple is so typical
As you can see I like my milky
Lovely chocolate
I might give it up, yeah right!

Ella Rutherford (9)
St Margaret's CE Primary School, Basildon

Ghost Cinquain

The ghost
Creepy and white
Says boo, big and see through
Peers through the door, gives a big fright
Haunted!

Lee Buckland (9)
St Margaret's CE Primary School, Basildon

The War Cinquain

The war
Dark forever
Raids everlasting shells
The noise intoxicating hell
Horrid.

Toby Blunsten (9)
St Margaret's CE Primary School, Basildon

My Chocolate Poem

Yum, yum, my favourite chocolate
Ripple melting in my mouth
Creamy chocolate, dreamy chocolate
I feel that I'm falling through the air
Without a care.
Toffee Crisp makes me lisp
Revels make me look like a devil,
Maltesers are for geezers
I like a Crunchie munchie
When I am not so happy.

Lauren Glover (9)
St Margaret's CE Primary School, Basildon

The Robber

Dark in the night when all is black
A robber is creeping around the back
Creaking doors and squeaky feet
Looking around at everything neat
Smashing cameras taking money
He really thinks he is funny
Soon to be rich? I think not
The police are coming
There are a lot.

Billy Ridgwell (9)
St Margaret's CE Primary School, Basildon

Vampire Cinquain

Sharp fangs
Loves bloodsucking
Creeps along corridors
Spine-chilling, shivering, shaking
Vampire.

Sam Everitt (9)
St Margaret's CE Primary School, Basildon

Monster?

There's a monster lurking under my bed
He has brown teeth and a shaggy head.
He is the monster from my nightmare,
He gives me a terrible scare.
My heart is drumming and drumming,
The monster's coming and coming,
All of a sudden my mum is there,
He must have heard her on the stair.
He disappears in the gloom,
Does he live in the corner of my room?
Was that monster really there
Or was he just a puff of air?
You decide.

Francesca Barnes (9)
St Margaret's CE Primary School, Basildon

The Old Lady From Ealing

There was an old lady from Ealing
Who had a peculiar feeling
She sat in the chair
With her cup of tea in the air
And it dribbled all over the ceiling.

Georgina Ames-Thompson (9)
St Margaret's CE Primary School, Basildon

The Young Man's Hat

There once was a young man's old hat
That looked incredibly fat
He loved it a lot
But felt very hot
So eventually he gave it to the cat.

Thomas Parkinson (9)
St Margaret's CE Primary School, Basildon

A Child's Dream

Caramel Twix,
Made for licks,
Turkish Delight
For those with the sight
It's in your fate
Have an After Eight
The Toffee Crisp
Adds the zist
The Jaffa cake
Keeps you awake,
The Kit-Kat
As eaten by Postman Pat.
The M&M
Eaten by Mr Sean Penn.
Aero,
Made in Rio de Janeiro.
For those with range,
Have a Terry's Orange.
Dairy Milk
Soft as silk,
And a Curly Wurly,
To keep you early.

Richard Kendall (10)
St Margaret's CE Primary School, Basildon

Foxy Kennings

Sly hunter
Night prowler
Sharp ears
Cub howler
Den hider
Red and browner.

Rebekah Stiff (9)
St Margaret's CE Primary School, Basildon

Chocolate Fever!

Celebrations in the morning, Miniature Heroes at night.
I like caramel and fudge as a midnight feast.
When it comes to chocolate, I turn into a beast,
Yorkie is not eaten with a forkie.
When I eat Snickers you can see my knickers.
Toffee goes great with coffee.
Fudge, fudge, fudge, when I eat it, I can't budge.

Have a sweet date with an After Eight,
Ripple, ripple, I can't live without it.
I'm a chocoholic as you can see, I would simply die without it.
Time Out, time to stop eating, I'm on a ban!

Yeah right!

Sarah Hurley (10)
St Margaret's CE Primary School, Basildon

Animal Poem

A snake that hisses sounds like kisses
A bear that roars likes to snore
A kangaroo that jumps likes to thump
A tiger that kills likes to thrill
A dog that growls likes to prowl.

Jack George Burton (9)
St Margaret's CE Primary School, Basildon

A Fish In The Sea

There was a fish in the sea
His name was Lee
He was sent to flee
For days and nights he travelled so far
And now he's in the fish bar.

Bradley Webb (9)
St Margaret's CE Primary School, Basildon

Chocolate Poem About Chocolate!

C adbury's caramel melts on your tongue
H ot chocolate soothes your throat
O pen wide smooth Galaxy inside
C ream eggs crunch in your mouth
O pen the wrapper and see the chocolate waiting for you
    to bite into it
L uscious lips bite into lovely Flake
A nnoying Twix gets in the mix
T erry's Chocolate Orange waits for a break
E very chocolate is lovely.

Amy Wallis (9)
St Margaret's CE Primary School, Basildon

Autumn Colours

Colours of autumn are brown and red
You will see lots of colours
When you get out of bed.
Search for things on the ground,
Like conkers and chestnuts sitting around.
Autumn days are wet but warm,
You won't see colours when the day is dawn.
Sticks and leaves on the trees,
All fall off in a gentle breeze.

Stewart Harvey (9)
St Margaret's CE Primary School, Basildon

The Man From France

There once was a man from France
Who always loved to dance
But one day he fell so hard you can tell
Because now he only can prance.

Daniella Kelt (9)
St Margaret's CE Primary School, Basildon

Limerick Help! I'm Stuck In A Pie!

There was a man from Dubai
Who fell into a twenty foot pie
He was covered in berry
Got stuck in jelly
And thought he was going to die.

Alex Barnes (9)
St Margaret's CE Primary School, Basildon

Limerick I Love Curry!

There was once a man from Surrey
Who ate lots and lots of curry
He ate vindaloo
From eleven till two
Then he filled his face with a McFlurry!

Joe Davies (9)
St Margaret's CE Primary School, Basildon

Incredibly Silly

There was a young boy called Willy
Who couldn't stop eating chilli
He had no hair
That's why he was bare
And he was incredibly silly.

Willis Smith (9)
St Margaret's CE Primary School, Basildon

A Kitten Cinquain

Kitten soft and furry
Laying in the sunshine
Pouncing on a mouse in the street
Purring.

Kate Box (10)
St Margaret's CE Primary School, Basildon

The Kind Lady

There was a very kind lady from Kent
Who liked to put up a tent
One day she went camping
Elephants came stamping
And all the poles were bent.

Molly Carter (9)
St Margaret's CE Primary School, Basildon

Lord Brocket

There was a man called Lord Brocket
Who went up in a rocket
His ears went clang
He went bang
And ended up in his pocket.

Conor Briden (9)
St Margaret's CE Primary School, Basildon

Mushroom Pot Scott

There was once a boy called Scott
Who lived in a mushroom pot
One day he got bored
So he prayed to the Lord
Then he ended up in a grey sock.

James Ball (9)
St Margaret's CE Primary School, Basildon

I Love Kittens

White kittens, black kittens and ginger ones too
They are soft and warm and cuddly too.
When we play, we play with a ball
They love climbing up the wall until they fall.

Rebecca Street (7)
St Margaret's CE Primary School, Basildon

Kennings Killer Whale

Fast swimmer
Dolphin killer
Black eyed
Cold skin
People scarer
Boat basher
Sea hunter
Fish eater
Sea king.

Patrick Smyth (9)
St Margaret's CE Primary School, Basildon

Winter

W hen it's cold I wrap up warm
 I ce is shiny and pointed
N ext the snow falls
T hrough the tree trunk a robin pops out
E ager for food
R un, robin run.

Rachel Everingham (9)
St Margaret's CE Primary School, Basildon

Fire!

Silent creeper
Blood burning
Gas lover
Petrol guzzler
Trace leaver
Disaster area
Elemental killer
   Fire!

Thomas Olson (9)
St Margaret's CE Primary School, Basildon

Chocolate Poem

I woke up in the morning and had a toffee
My daughter brought me up a coffee
I ate a Mars,
It took me to the stars,
I had some Maltesers,
Up popped some geezers,
After I had a Toblerone,
My son said 'On your own!'
Then I had a posh date,
With an After Eight,
Time Out, time to stop eating,
I'm on a bam, yeah right!

George Watts (11)
St Margaret's CE Primary School, Basildon

There Was A Young Man From Bath

There was a young man from Bath
Wherever he went he took a scarf,
But never a hat,
Nor a cat
And everybody thought he was daft.

Justine Turbin (10)
St Margaret's CE Primary School, Basildon

Poor Boy

There was a young boy from Devon
Whose mum died and went up to Heaven
The young boy cried
As his mother had died
And the poor boy was only seven.

Jimmy Wilson (10)
St Margaret's CE Primary School, Basildon

Island Cinquain

Island
Delicious fruit
Monkeys swinging from trees
See the deer and antelope play
Relax!

Ben Couch (10)
St Margaret's CE Primary School, Basildon

The Knights Coloured Death March

All ye knights of ye old age,
Raise your swords and show us your blades,
Out of the brown book we shall take a page,
We will strike at night in the moonlight's silver shade,
From the greyest mist of the fog,
We travel in silence through the dark green bog,
Attack we will at the golden walls,
In our bright blue tunics we don't look like fools,
Destroy their walls, with fire so red,
None will be left standing, they'll all be left dead.

Scott Smith (11)
St Margaret's CE Primary School, Basildon

Rush Hour Cinquain

Rush hour
Cars speed along
Traffic never ceasing
People rush to work all morning
Traffic.

Joe Kelt (10)
St Margaret's CE Primary School, Basildon

Weather

The rain comes strongly all of this night
Pitter-patter what a fright
It gives the people in the town
A heavy face and a grumpy frown.

The sun however as bright as could be
Drying up the rain and sea
We're always pleased to see the sun
It brings us joy and lots of fun!

Eloise Taylor (10)
St Margaret's CE Primary School, Basildon

What Is It?

Quick pacer,
Food racer,
Silk spinner,
Leggy winner,
Confuses dinner,
Egg layer,
Widow forever!

(Black Widow Spider.)

Paige Headon (10)
St Margaret's CE Primary School, Basildon

Dark Heaven

Wrapper of gold and silver
Chocolate so good you get a shiver
Mint and orange all for you
Don't forget that caramel goo
White and milk chocolate
Make the dark Heaven.

Joseph McAreavey (10)
St Margaret's CE Primary School, Basildon

Seasons

Autumn is the time of year
When leaves fall on the ground with fear
The wind blows fast
And then at last . . .

Winter is the time of year
When rainy weather's nearly here
The snow falls down
All over town
And then it's the beginning of . . .

Spring comes only once a year
And blossom starts to form
The flowers start to grow again
And then it's the beginning of . . .

Summer is the time of year
When all the weather's hot
The birds sing clearly in your ears
And all the seasons start again!

Nicolle Morris (10)
St Margaret's CE Primary School, Basildon

Kennings Diary

Secret keeper
Best friend
Refresher
Personal belonging
Note taker
Special listener
Date finder
No one knows.

It's a diary.

Lauren Stanton (10)
St Margaret's CE Primary School, Basildon

Chocolate Rap

I like my Taxis
With my Kinder Maxis
After my meat
I have my Quality Street
Maltesers the perfect pleasers
Stop! Gateau Time!

Engine, engine on a chocolate line
On the New York Galaxy line
If my Aero goes off the tracks
Put it in, put it in, put it in, in ya mouth
A - o ro-lo a - o ro-lo.

Do you want a Creme Egg, Twix or Mars
How about a Dream or Milky Way Stars
Eat chocolate all day, be sick in the morning
So I don't go to school (oh it's so boring).

Sam Garnett (11)
St Margaret's CE Primary School, Basildon

Yellow

The sun is yellow
It burns bright
A sunflower yellow
It grows in daylight
A daffodil is yellow
They grow and they grow
Mustard is yellow
But don't eat it though
The sand is yellow
It stays on the ground.

Emma Mustafa (11)
St Margaret's CE Primary School, Basildon

My Teacher

Discipline maker
Education giver
Desk sitter
Coffee drinker
Spelling checker
Voice shouter
Teampoint giver
Playground watcher.

Tyra King (10)
St Margaret's CE Primary School, Basildon

Sunset

S unset, oh sunset
U nder the great coloured sky
N ever have I seen such a beautiful sight
S unset, oh sunset
E verlasting we hope, but only for minutes, then you will set
T he sky is empty without you sunset.

Megan Pascoe (10)
St Margaret's CE Primary School, Basildon

My Snow Limerick

There once was a snowman called Fred,
Whose mum and dad were both dead.
In the hot summer's sun,
Their days were done
And all that was left was one head.

David Pringle (10)
St Margaret's CE Primary School, Basildon

Kennings

Human tracer
Invisible footsteps
Silent speaker
Immortal observer
Nightmare checker.

Painting.

Lawrence Mount (10)
St Margaret's CE Primary School, Basildon

Snow

Snow is glistening
While people are listening,
To the falling snow,
With a great glow,
Let's have a snowball fight,
But not at night.

Adam Peake (11)
St Margaret's CE Primary School, Basildon

There Was A Young Lady From Kent

There was a young lady from Kent
Who had a rather big tent
She fell in her car
And went pretty far
And we will never see her again.

Angelica Hood (10)
St Margaret's CE Primary School, Basildon

Take Cover!

A dull black looking for cover in a shadow,
A shy black looking for a dark place to hide,
An elegant black shivering in fright behind a rock,
A splendour black moving with the night, to try and lose it,
They will never get away from it, it's coming, it's here!
A dark and evil black, wiping out the others,
Nothing has defeated it and nothing ever will!

Jasmin Palmer (11)
St Margaret's CE Primary School, Basildon

Winter

Winter is here
The sun hasn't appeared.

No one has won the snowball fights
So they fly their kite.

It's snowing today
The children are out to play.

James Lund (11)
St Margaret's CE Primary School, Basildon

The Boy From Leicester

There was a young boy with a Fiesta
Who lived with his mother in Leicester
He loved to get dressed
But he was always a mess
So they left him in Leicester.

Jack Mitchell (11)
St Margaret's CE Primary School, Basildon

My Uncle Fred

My uncle Fred
went to bed
and dreamt he was dancing away,
but when he woke up
he heard a hiccup
and he found his dog had gone astray.

Rachel McArdell (8)
St Margaret's CE Primary School, Basildon

Scary Night

I was on duty in the guard room
When a skeleton rode in on a broom,
So I squirted shampoo,
And showered him with glue.
But he couldn't be real, I presume
Luckily he didn't drag me away to my doom.

Joe Turbin (8)
St Margaret's CE Primary School, Basildon

Snow

Snow is so bright
That it shines at night
It glitters when the sun is light
It is like loads and loads of powder
And tastes very sour.

Luke Amis (7)
St Margaret's CE Primary School, Basildon

Brownies

Brownies is fun
We play games and run
We make cards and display
For special day
We go on trips on the bus
And Brown Owl looks after us all day.

Amy Coles (7)
St Margaret's CE Primary School, Basildon

Ghosts

Ghosts are creepy they are scary too
They live in people's houses
To creep around the room
They hide in your wardrobe
To come and spook you
When you sleep at night.

Adam Coles (7)
St Margaret's CE Primary School, Basildon

The Loud Man

There was an old man from France
Who sang very loud to the plants
The plants did wilt so
He put on a kilt
And tried a funny dance.

Adam Tucker (9)
St Margaret's CE Primary School, Basildon

Surprise Cinquain

Surprise
Wrapped with blue tape
At a birthday party
Give your friends an invitation
Have fun.

Paul Oliphant (10)
St Margaret's CE Primary School, Basildon

Wonderful Day, Worrying Night

All day I wonder through the woods,
I have done all my life.
I wouldn't trade a single thing,
I love the way I live
The way I live loves me.

Night draws near
Soon my day will sink beneath
My world.

The sky is dark
My friends the trees revisit
And terrify my mind
As if they were monsters
In my heart I can see them drawing in
I am so breathless nearly in my death.

I cannot explain the way I feel.

Once again the day I lived,
Day in day out has arrived
But I still know that tonight
I will have to live that
Dream once again.

Vicky Eves (10)
St Mary Magdalen Primary School, King's Lynn

You Never Know

You may think
You are too young to die
But you never know
When you go to sleep
You might think
You'll wake up
All cheerful
But you never know.

You are old
You think you are going to die
You never know
You might have an illness
You think you are going to die
You never know.

Your time has come
Now you are dead
You might come back as something else
You never know.

Jake Fenn (9)
St Mary Magdalen Primary School, King's Lynn

Friends 'n' Enemies

Friends are loving companions
Friends never let you down
They'll always be your partner
And will help when you breakdown.

Enemies are insulting
Enemies are disrespectful
They never think before they say
But they won't always be so hurtful.

Jodie Button (10)
St Mary Magdalen Primary School, King's Lynn

Over The Sea

Sea horses dashing
Angrily in the tide
Harbour boats smashing
Waves roll on the seaside
People take cover
From the wild stormy night
Animals shiver
It's almost struck midnight.

Over the North Sea
All is very peaceful
Children playing Frisbee
People here are cheerful
The sun is shining
Perfectly in the sky.

Daryl Waters (9)
St Mary Magdalen Primary School, King's Lynn

The ABC

The ABC is not for me,
I don't get the D and I
Don't get the E
Can't all the letters see
I don't get on with the ABC!

I want to get on with the letters you see
And I think that school is the key,
To learn my numeracy and literacy,
I can get on with the ABC.

Now I can and will be,
A clever student in University,
Though I still have to pay my fee
At least I'll know my . . .

ABC!

Katherine Jones (10)
St Mary Magdalen Primary School, King's Lynn

Ill And Well

I remember playing
Home from school, scoffing tea
Staying out as long as possible
Repeatedly.

Now,
I can barely walk
I can't climb stairs
Looking back
At what I could do
Brings tears to my eyes.

If only
If only
I could still
Do that.
If the disease
Hadn't taken over
My life.

Jamie Marks (10)
St Mary Magdalen Primary School, King's Lynn

Hell And Heaven

Hell is disaster
Heaven is God
Hell is scorching
Heaven is angels
Hell is abandoned
Heaven is extraordinary
Hell is the Devil
Heaven is life
Hell is extreme death
Heaven is ethereal.

Jamie Hart (10)
St Mary Magdalen Primary School, King's Lynn

I, Too

(Based on 'I, Too' by Langston Hughes)

I too, am like you
I eat and play like you,
even if I am the slave of you.
I may call you Master,
you may call me slave
But I am strong,
I shall live my life.

Tomorrow
I will get you back
Somehow,
Some way,
I shall not call you Master,
You shall not call me slave,
Nobody will,
Not even you.

Besides,
They'll see how courageous I am

And be amazed

I too, am like you.

Rebecca Gipp (11)
St Mary Magdalen Primary School, King's Lynn

Heaven And Hell

Heaven is Jesus
Hell is wreckage
Heaven is happiness
Hell is blazing
Heaven is a dream
Hell is a regret
Heaven is crowded
Hell is Hades.

Max Rossiter (11)
St Mary Magdalen Primary School, King's Lynn

One Day One Night!

On this scorching day
Adults are saying
That the sea is playing
With the children in the gleaming sand.

On this starless night
A shark will devour
Anyone who comes
But
Do not fear
Lifeguards are here
To save you from its jaws.

Jake Reed (10)
St Mary Magdalen Primary School, King's Lynn

Move 'n' Groove

Nothing's better than a person's groove
Come now and watch them move,
You should get this lot moving
This music is really grooving.

Can't get better than a woman here
Really, honestly you should fear,
Come on now let's move your feet
Keep going and catch the beat.

Now it's on the music won't stop going,
Now the music is completely flowing,
This really is a late night swing
Let's keep on going and do our thing!

Ross Lucie-Smith (11)
St Mary Magdalen Primary School, King's Lynn

I, Too

(Based on 'I, Too' by Langston Hughes)

I, too, am human
I can't help being disabled
People push me
And call me names
But I still make friends.

Tomorrow
I will stand up for myself
They will understand
What it is like to live in a wheelchair.

Besides, they will see me
As I am
I, too, am human.

Holly Eastwood (10)
St Mary Magdalen Primary School, King's Lynn

I, Too

(Based on 'I, Too' by Langston Hughes)

I, too, am part of you
I will not let you boss me around
I am a different colour
But you cannot stop me
From doing the things I do.

Tomorrow,
You will see through the colour of my skin
And what I really am
Dreams don't come true.

I, too, am part of you.

Katy Flett (9)
St Mary Magdalen Primary School, King's Lynn

The Storm

The wild raging storm is an angry giant
Terrifying lightning bolts through the sky like
Fiery weapons as it thunders.
Voice frightens and echoes furiously.
The wind shrieks like a screaming girl.
Its icy hands grip the house tightly as a tiger's claw.
The rain beats furiously against the window like shells
Inside, the fire greets us as friends and we feel warm
And snug as a hibernating hedgehog.

Daniel Rains (11)
St Mary Magdalen Primary School, King's Lynn

The Cat And His Witch

On a night as black as coal,
Where the full moon looms
And stars are scattered carelessly
The soft padding of silky feet
Can be heard.
In the darkest silence eyes
Green and burning can be glimpsed.
Through shadows of darkness
The creature's ears prick,
To the sound of distant wailing
As the witch calls the cat
But the cat simply purrs and
Spreads out his whiskers.
As the cat refuses to obey her call
For many people are happy to tell,
The witch does not own the cat.

The cat owns the witch.

Morgan Creed (11)
Sacred Heart Convent School, Swaffham

The Stationary Faerie

I'd like to see a stationary faerie
But I don't think I ever will,
For it's commonly known in the faerie world
That a faerie never stands still.

I might never see a faerie
Still or not, until I'm old,
Faeries don't like naughty children -
I'll have to do as I'm told.

It was Christmas Eve in England
How I tried to shut my eyes!
I lay alone with just my thoughts,
When I saw some fireflies.

They were darting about the cuckoo clock
As it struck the twelfth eerie hour,
They shot through the air like shooting stars,
While in the corner I cowered.

When the twelfth cry had echoed and died,
I gazed at them in wondrous shock,
The cuckoo was blind to the luck he was granted -
Faeries were resting on his clock!

I dared to move closer and closer still,
I saw their golden wings,
I saw their long hair, floating about,
I touched their Faerie King.

Then I felt a warming sensation
Rush through my body; I'd seen . . .
A whole clan of stationary faeries
And become their Faerie Queen!

Rosalind Peters (11)
Sacred Heart Convent School, Swaffham

My Rainbow

I had a wonderful pony
Her lovely golden mane
I loved her with all my heart
I wish I could see her again.

She lay in the field
In the hot summer sun
When all her hard work
Was over and done.

But now she's in Heaven
She's gone far away
But I'll love her forever
Till the end of my days.

For when that day comes
We'll be together again.

Amy Stevens (11)
Sacred Heart Convent School, Swaffham

Pony Poem

When you look out of the window
And all you see is a little pony waiting to be.

Do we expect it? No we don't
So what do we do? Well I don't know.

So all we do is act as normal
Looking at the pony under the tree,
Perhaps by the time we wake up tomorrow
There will be the foal that was waiting to be.

Beccy Case (11)
Sacred Heart Convent School, Swaffham

All About Cats

Cats are beautiful creatures,
Such elegant features.
With their dainty paws
And neatly clipped claws.

Their lovely coats of silk
Which they do not splash when they lap up their milk.
Their lovely eyes as green as glass,
Are as shiny as polished brass.

Their tiny teeth as white as pearls,
They never bite a soul, especially not girls.
And their little tongues that are pink like roses,
Are the same colour as the end of their noses.

They have such a gentle nature,
Oh I do love cats!

Bronwen Brewer (11)
Sacred Heart Convent School, Swaffham

Our Brain

Have you ever wondered what's inside your brain?
Is there a miniature filing cabinet
Containing all the words you ever learnt?

Nobody really knows what's hidden inside your head,
Only you.

Are there hundreds of little people,
Working tirelessly,
Tidying away all your thoughts and memories
Before they get lost?

Nobody knows what's inside your brain,
Nobody ever will.

Sophie Prentis (10)
Sacred Heart Convent School, Swaffham

Daffodils

Spring daffodils are budding now
Peering up through the grass
To see whether it is time to come out yet
In late February there will be a sea of yellow in the garden.
Daffodils waving on the side of the road and in the park
Dotted everywhere like a spotted quilt.
Daffodils dance in the wind with the birds singing in the background.
There are crowds of pearly snowdrops crowding round in amazement
The colour of the daffodils is as bright as the sun and as
                                                    bright as a light.
In the beginning they were as tall as a soldier but now in the
                                          end their heads are drooping
I look forward to seeing their golden heads again next year.

Sarah Johnson (11)
Sacred Heart Convent School, Swaffham

Spring

Spring is almost here, it's nearly my birthday,
All the bunnies bouncing
All the buds opening,
Easter eggs being eaten
Spring is the best time of the year
Spring brings nature from afar
There are bright colours in spring
Pink, yellow, white and green
Sometimes there's a light breeze
Sometimes there's no breeze at all.

Megan Hook (10)
Sacred Heart Convent School, Swaffham

The Dog Below The Window sill

As I gaze down upon the garden
The family dog approaches my window sill
I hiss angrily and arch my back
Still the dog does not back off,
though it edges closer!
There is something strange about the dog's eyes;
almost mesmerising.
I can see in the dog's eyes
It wants to bite me, but I cannot move my body.
My tail is hanging loosely over the edge of the window sill.
The dog's eyes shift from mine and focus on my tail
and I see its mouth start to open.
I jump from the window sill onto the dog's back
and sink my claws into it.
Before the dog can bite me I am away into the nearby hedge,
victory over the dog at last!

Sophie Morgan-Short (10)
Sacred Heart Convent School, Swaffham

My Summer Poem

It's the season of summer, my birthday is coming up
I wonder what I'll get I might get a tiny pup.
I can't wait to see all the flowers blooming
All the birds getting ready for their tuning.
All the animals are enjoying the dry ground,
All the cattle are running round
All the birds are singing loudly
All the children running madly
I like the season of summer
It's the greatest season ever.

Emily Chaffer (11)
Sacred Heart Convent School, Swaffham

Seasons

Bright spring colours
Colourful spring flowers
New leaves are forming
The wind is calling.

The wind is in the trees
The fat furry bumblebees
Are searching for nectar
And pollen
The wind is calling.

Hannah Coggles (10)
Sacred Heart Convent School, Swaffham

The Four Seasons!

Spring
In the spring lambs are born
Flowers blooming in the dawn.
It's time for the birds to make their nest
It's time for the hedgehogs to end their rest!

Summer
In the summer children say,
'Hooray hooray it's time to play!'
The grass is lush and getting longer,
The trees are green and getting stronger.

Autumn
In the autumn we have fireworks and fun
But for some people it makes them run!
Golden leaves fall from the trees
Children love to play with these!

Winter
In the winter north winds blow
Bringing lots of frost and snow!
Christmas comes and best of all,
Dear old Santa comes to call!

Alice Harness (9)
Wimbotsham Primary School, King's Lynn

Cuddly Dudley

A friend like you,
Is always there,
White and black,
I really care.

I love you from all
My heart's desire,
You're really small
My best friend too.

You don't judge me
You're really mind,
What I do,
You never mind.

You're the brother
I'd really like
You're no bother
Full of love.

Wet black nose
Soft and cuddly
You're my comfort blanket
This is my Dudley.

What am I?

Holly Bloy (10)
Wimbotsham Primary School, King's Lynn

Without A Care

The touch of rain
On the long black mane
The sound of the thunder
From the hooves down under
The wind through my hair
You had to be there
That feeling of freedom on my favourite mare.

Fiona Thompson (11)
Wimbotsham Primary School, King's Lynn

Katy's Rabbit

Katy had a rabbit
A naughty rabbit she had
A funny name this is
She named her rabbit Dad!

Katy's rabbit is a very naughty rabbit
Indeed,
He is so naughty
He gobbles up the weeds.

Now this rabbit digs up holes
He eats the neighbour's bowls,
The neighbours weren't happy
The rabbit ate the baby's nappy.

Ellen Atkinson-Legge (9)
Wimbotsham Primary School, King's Lynn

Summer

Summer is cool
I get to go in the pool
It's nice and hot
I wish it wouldn't stop.

We have loads of barbecues
No one argues
We sunbathe in the sun
And have loads of fun

Summer is the best season
No one can beat him.

Alex Grant (10)
Wimbotsham Primary School, King's Lynn

Cup Winnin' Team

We're fast, runnin'
Leg breakin'
Good shootin'
Great defendin'
Ball smashin'
Excellent keepin'
Brilliant strikin'
Great field in'
High jumpin'
Mad celebratin'
Fast dribblin'
Cool tacklin'
Bad managin'
Hard kickin'
Quick passin'

Cup Winnin' Team.

Liam Thorpe (10)
Wimbotsham Primary School, King's Lynn

Dogs

Dogs are fluffy,
Dogs are furry,
Dogs are long,
Dogs are strong.

Dogs are short,
So I was taught,
Dogs are big
Most of them dig.

Most are sweet,
Some just sleep
But all are nice
No matter what the price.

Chelsea Ryan (11)
Wimbotsham Primary School, King's Lynn

The Mystery Horse

It trots and gallops across the plane
With no one holding its leather rein
His pure white coat shines in the sun
Every evening he starts to run.

He listens to the steam, and the creaking of the track
He feels the ghost riding on his bare back.
The gentle push of the black-masked guy,
That was before he actually did die.

The horse, he trotted quickly up to the track,
And still there was no one riding on his back.
It was the same, as when his owner was shot,
And soon the horse stopped his trot.

Ever since that day, the horse ran away
And never was seen again.

Hollie Newling (10)
Wimbotsham Primary School, King's Lynn

Quickly

Quickly, the sea speeds up the sand
Quickly, the spider runs down the hand
Quickly, the bird flew across the sky
Quickly, the lightning begins to fly.

Quickly, the rain falls from the roof,
Quickly, the jacket becomes waterproof.
Quickly, the snake slithers through the tree
Quickly, he comes and sees, to frighten me.

Sophie Guttridge (11)
Wimbotsham Primary School, King's Lynn

My Family And Me

My name is Jedd and I am a pain when it is time for bed
I don't like to go, so I say, 'Noooooooo.'

My youngest brother is Jordan and his mouth flows like the
                                        River Jordan,
He non-stop talks until he goes to sleep and tumbles into a heap.

My other brother Jae is always far away, he daydreams all day.
He is into Power Rangers but can't stand strangers.

My big sister Shannan has a mouth bigger than a cannon!
She always rants and raves and screams for days and days
But that's just her way!

My dad, he is a very funny lad, he has a big belly and can be
Rather smelly especially if he doesn't wear spray.
He wobbles all day just like a melted Milky Way.

My mum is a midget and constantly fidgets,
She can't sit still even behind the wheel,
But God can she cook a good meal!

We have five snakes which escape then make us shake and quake,
We also have a Rotty that can be quite dotty and even a little potty.

So all in all that is my family and me,
My next poem will be about my family tree.

Jedd Desborough (8)
Wimbotsham Primary School, King's Lynn